Student-Driven Learning

Small, medium, and big steps
to engage and empower students

JENNIFER HARPER

KATHRYN O'BRIEN

Pembroke Publishers Limited

Dedications

To Samuel, whose never-ending questions are a testament to the wonderment of learning.—KO

To Casey, for his support, and to Dean and Jack, who made a book in one day and wondered why it took Mommy so much longer.—JH

© **2012 Pembroke Publishers**
538 Hood Road
Markham, Ontario, Canada L3R 3K9
www.pembrokepublishers.com

Distributed in the U.S. by Stenhouse Publishers
480 Congress Street
Portland, ME 04101
www.stenhouse.com

We acknowledge the financial support of the Government of Canada through the Book Publishing Industry Development Program (BPIDP) for our publishing activities.

We acknowledge the assistance of the Government of Ontario through the Ontario Media Development Corporation's Ontario Book Initiative.

Library and Archives Canada Cataloguing in Publication

Harper, Jennifer
    Student-driven learning : small, medium, and big steps to engage and empower students / Jennifer Harper, Kathryn O'Brien.

Includes bibliographical references and index.
Issued also in electronic format.
ISBN 978-1-55138-278-4

    1. Student-centered learning. 2. Active learning. 3. Education, Elementary. I. O'Brien, Kathryn Ellen II. Title.

LB1027.23.H37 2012   371.39   C2012-903957-8

eBook format ISBN 978-1-55138-846-5
Editor: Kat Mototsune
Cover Design: John Zehethofer
Typesetting: Jay Tee Graphics Ltd.

Printed and bound in Canada
9 8 7 6 5 4 3 2 1

MIX
Paper from
responsible sources
FSC® C004071

Contents

Introduction

Education-as-usual assumes that kids are empty vessels who need to be sat down in a room and filled with curricular content. Dr. Mitra's experiments prove that wrong.

—Doc Searls, "Natural Curiosity" (2002)

In the urban slums of New Delhi, Sugata Mitra installed an Internet-connected PC in a hole in the wall. Following the activities of the children through a hidden camera, Mitra and his colleagues watched what happened when children were given free rein. Their natural curiosity took over and within weeks many of the children were computer literate and had begun to teach other children from the neighborhood. Sugata Mitra went on to repeat this experiment in urban and rural areas throughout India and the results were always the same. Children will be inspired to learn in the right conditions and with the right stimulus.

This story would not surprise many educators—we have all observed what happens in our classrooms when students are provided with a compelling problem and discovery time. But as educators we are caught between worlds. We are locked into a system we need to follow and report on. We need to meet our curricular expectations, as well as the many new programs thrust into our agendas. We often feel we cannot cover the expectations in the limited time we have. We don't have time to wonder why certain systems exist or to ponder the value of the expectations we are struggling to meet. We are trapped by curriculum objectives, testing, understaffing, lack of resources, lack of time, classroom discipline, parental concerns…and the list continues to grow. This book is not about adding to the list; rather it is about looking critically at how to engage and support our students in discovery, problem-solving, and, most importantly, igniting the fire for lifelong learning.

With the influx of digital technology, the world is changing. The ways in which we communicate and share information are changing. We are the digital immigrants and our students are the digital natives; we are trying to navigate through their world. What's more, we are trying to determine what skills our students need and how we can teach them. We are struggling to catch up and be the bearers of knowledge in a world where information is no longer static. If we cannot trust time-honored habits of thinking and doing, how do we understand the nature of our teaching practice? We are trapped in the overwhelming pressure of preparing our students for an unknown future, all the while looking into their world and trying to bring out the excitement, wonders, and magic of learning.

We are preparing our students for jobs that do not currently exist, to use technologies that have not been invented, to solve problems that we don't even know are problems yet. As educators we are entering a time when the former ideas of pedagogy no longer suffice.

OUR WORLD

- The U.S. Department of Labor estimates that today's learner will have 10–14 jobs by the age of 38.
- The top in-demand jobs of 2010 did not exist in 2004.
- As of December 2011, there are more than 800 million registered Facebook users.
- There are more than 12 billion searches on Google each month.
- The number of text messages sent and received every day exceeds the total population of the planet.
- More than 4000 new books are being published every day.
- It is estimated that 40 exabytes of new information will be generated worldwide this year.
- 228 million laptops and tablets were shipped worldwide this year.

(Rose et al., 2012)

Our new digital era also opens a world of possibilities—literally. We are becoming more global. We are interacting with peers around the world, instantly and easily. We no longer need to rely on formal channels for acquiring knowledge. On a global scale, anyone can express an opinion; all people can add their ideas and publish their thoughts. In this new world we take action to help ourselves and others we feel are in need. Using digital media, we can gather, rise up, show strength, and affect social change. Knowledge is fluid; we all add to and take from this global knowledge pool.

Why do we need to shift to student-driven learning?

> Students 10 years from now will be less self-motivated, less creative and less excited about learning. [We] worry that future students will think if something isn't on a test, it doesn't matter…. This could kill innovation. Company executives bred on bubble answers would stick closely to what they know and what's been done, possibly latching on to a new idea here and there but rarely having their own. Medical research would stall; advances in technology would stumble. Poems and novels would languish undiscovered in the brains of our young people…This would stifle the economy by crushing creativity and drive. (Muzslay, 2004)

There is a growing awareness that a conventional education system, one in which we provide our students with all information, is not meeting the needs of our changing world. Our students are not thinking critically about the world around them. Our students are memorizing facts and data for outdated tests. This means we need to shift our practice. Educators are looking for solutions, looking for ways to prepare their students for unknown futures. As a result, student-driven learning is becoming more prominent in conversations in and out of the classroom.

In addition to preparing for the future, we are also seeking ways to engage and motivate our students in the present. We need to get our students passionate about learning while they are still in school. We also need to recognize that learning has become more fluid, more independent, and more informal. We can no longer hold to the structured classroom where the teacher knows all. Our students are the drivers—their daily experience is their reality and what they are doing now matters. We need to create an environment that motivates, empowers, challenges, and pushes our students now so that they engage in their current experience and are prepared for the future.

Acknowledgments

We'd like to thank...

Our students, whose exuberance and energy helped drive this book into fruition. When we turned over the ownership of the learning from our hands to theirs, we saw a shift in motivation and engagement that was impossible to ignore. Our students remind us everyday that learning is a journey where everyone gets a turn at the wheel.

Mary Macchiusi and Kat Mototsune for their collaboration and patience with us as we delved into this adventure, and for giving us the opportunity to share our love of being in the classroom.

Our friends for giving us the nourishment (both through ideas and good food) to write this book, and our parents for being our most powerful teachers and guides.

All our professional friends for sharing their teaching experiences and classrooms with us. Special thanks to Lisa Fleming, Carly Crippin, Rebecca Ryder, Lara Jensen, Chris Roy, Christine Keene, Laura Heyes, Geremy Vincent, Nancy Preston, Karyn McCormack, Erica Sprules, and Christina Morgan-Poort.

1

How to Put Students in the Driver's Seat

> Imagine a world where everyone was constantly learning, a world where what you wondered was more interesting than what you knew, and curiosity counted for more than certain knowledge. Imagine a world where what you gave away was more valuable than what you held back, where joy was not a dirty word, where play was not forbidden after your eleventh birthday. Imagine a world in which the business of business was to imagine worlds people might actually want to live in someday. Imagine a world created by the people, for the people not perishing from the earth forever.
>
> Yeah. Imagine that.
>
> — Christopher Locke, *The Cluetrain Manifesto* (Levine et al, 2000)

There is a Chinese proverb: *Tell me and I'll forget; show me and I may remember; involve me and I'll understand.*

According to this way of thinking, our students have been in the driver's seat for centuries. Our children learn by immersing themselves in their experiences. They feel proud when they design, create, and accomplish a task. If they truly understand a concept and link it to other experiences, they feel a sense of empowerment over their learning, their knowledge, and where they want to drive next.

What is student-driven learning? Over time, this term has been used to cover such concepts as student-centred learning, student-directed learning, and flexible learning. In student-driven learning, students are active participants in their education. A classroom that uses student-driven learning fosters autonomy and shifts the focus from the knowledge and influence of the teacher to the experiences of the students, ultimately encouraging students to take the driver's seat in their own education.

Consider this: someone could tell me how to make cookies. I could read and study about making cookies. But it is not until I actually make the cookies themselves that I will learn what those descriptions of texture, taste, and aroma truly mean. Student-driven learning is creating the opportunities for our students to learn their own way, to take initiative, and to experience, wonder, and create in order to truly understand.

But do we have the resources or time to allow each child to make their own cookies or explore at their own rate? How would my classroom work if every child created his or her own learning plan? How do I manage this? We know that our students love to explore and learn. There are many studies that have shown students learn best by exploring. But how do we make this possible with 30 students; with 30 different needs, learning styles, backgrounds; with one small room and just a teacher in the front? The answer is this: we go back to the Chinese proverb and we involve our students in their own learning.

Elements of Student-Driven Learning

In addition to a chapter on each of the elements of student-driven learning, the chapter The Learning Map deals with how to unify and bring the elements of student-driven learning into your classroom. Using the tools of planning and assessment as guides, we outline how to create a unit that can bring student-driven learning to life.

This book is broken into six elements of student-driven learning. These elements do not work alone, nor do they come in a particular order. Our traditional teaching needs—curriculum objectives, planning, assessment—are not forgotten or minimized; rather they are embraced in each element. These elements are not the goals but the essence of this educational movement. By beginning with whichever element fits comfortably, we make steps toward engaging and empowering our students.

Taking a New Direction in Our Teaching Practice

Expectations of teachers reflect their culture, and the extent of a teacher's knowledge and skills relates to the environment in which they teach. Over the centuries, teachers have had to possess an understanding of complex military strategies, dexterous writing skills, extensive knowledge of biblical texts, an ability to stoke a fire in a coal-burning stove, and so on. What do teachers need to possess today to be knowledgeable and skilled for their students? If being knowledgeable means that a teacher possesses a memory that works like an Internet search engine, we are grasping at the impossible. If being skilled means that we are intimately familiar with the technological advances in our students' lives, we have never been more ignorant.

The idea that, as teachers, we are all-knowing sages with the maps to the learning process is a myth. Adopting the student-driven learning approach causes educators to reflect on their practice. We look beyond the curriculum and home in on student interest. We open our ideas of assessment, classroom management, and classroom design. The biggest shift is that we are no longer the bearers of knowledge in our classroom. The role of expert is shared among teachers and students. Teachers act more as meddlers in students' learning: we pose questions, scenarios, and activities that require student interaction and involvement. We are as actively engaged in the learning process as the students and act to provide support and direction through "hands on, minds on" learning experiences (Brown, 2005).

Knowing Our Students

As we shift from the position of teacher to that of fellow learner, we also deepen our knowledge of the learner. Truly knowing our students, their interests and strengths, helps create a classroom of learners. We foster what they can do and empower them to extend themselves to learn new things. To start, we reevaluate what we know about our students and what we believe about intelligence to deepen their possibilities. In professional jargon, this relationship is called "relational teaching" (Kitchen, 2005). In our everyday teaching world, it is ensuring that our students know we care about them, that we want to know them as individuals, and that we "get them."

Fueling the Spark

"If you are not prepared to be wrong, you will never come up with anything original. "
— Ken Robinson , *The Element* (2009)

Having the confidence to make mistakes is an important life skill. Through making mistakes, we figure out how to solve problems, how to evaluate what strategies work, and what not to do again. It is how we learn deeply and understand how to problem-solve.

In a classroom where the teacher works to create similarities rather than celebrate the differences, mistakes and errors are often seen as a failure; students learn quickly to stick to the status quo. Following instructions, copying the teacher, and providing the single best answer will ensure fewer embarrassments and often praise. While students may feel a temporary security in the classroom, the inevitable mistake or error can quickly disintegrate any feelings of confidence. Over time, this lack of confidence can create anxiety and even depression in our students.

The most important motivators to learning are intrinsic passion and an interest in the work itself (Adams, 2006). External pressures, such as getting the highest test scores, parental pride, teacher expectations, and prizes, can be very successful in encouraging a student. While these pressures might provide a short-term focus on achievement, they do not promote a long-term love of learning and passion for knowledge. When we make a priority of increasing student engagement, rather than improving test scores, we can actually foster greater gains in students' academic, emotional, social, and behavioral achievement (Klem & Connell, 2004). By transferring the classroom power to our students through small, medium, or big steps, we are telling them that we believe in them. We trust their judgment and we respect their opinions. This feeling of trust opens the door to new possibilities. It is an environment that students thrive in, a space where they can be free to create, explore, and wonder without judgment.

Getting Off the Linear Path

Do we expect our students to describe the feudal system at length years after they have completed their classroom project? Can we accurately recite learning that occurred in our early years? No. When we need information, we do what we know best: we research, use the Internet, collaborate, and connect previous ideas, and we figure it out. These skills are what we are teaching our students, not the structure of the feudal system or the order of the solar system—they can Google that. In our digital world, we have the tools to answer the *what* questions easily. We want our students to know how to find the information, understand it, apply it to their current understanding, and think critically about what they learn. We want our students to be the bearers of knowledge.

A PARADIGM SHIFT

Teachers as the Bearers of Knowledge	Students as the Bearers of Knowledge
• Passive transmission of knowledge from the teacher	• Active learning by the student
• Teacher chooses what information all students are required to know, with a focus on high grades and skill development	• Students pursue areas of individual interest, with a focus on whole-child development

• Students sit quietly and absorb teacher's information	• Students interact and talk with teacher and other students to find the best answer
• Students each create the same piece of work, modelled by the teacher with high expectations	• Students create individualized pieces of work demonstrating what they learned with the same high expectations
• Students are told how to solve a problem	• Students test and try ways to solve the problem, finding the best solution
• Focus on completing the task	• Focus on deeply understanding the task

Fostering the Creative Mindset

In its report *Tough Choices or Tough Times* the National Center for Education and the Economy pointed out that if educators want to create successful citizens of the 21st century, they must foster creativity within their students. As educators, we would be remiss if we continued to think of creativity as applying to only the most artistic student in the classroom. Our conventional classrooms do little to encourage creativity. Frequently, students come to understand that there is a single best answer; to achieve this answer you need a certain skill set and must follow a certain path. In contrast, a classroom that adopts student-driven learning is one that celebrates novelty and invention. Student innovation is welcomed and students are encouraged to pursue areas of self-interest. The emphasis on divergent and inventive thinking, as well as on collaboration and intrinsic motivation, is a petri dish for creative thought.

Diving into a Deeper Understanding

Imagine a new unit of study has begun, the much-anticipated Ancient Egypt unit. As a student, you are eager to learn and excited by the unique artifacts; you recall in great detail tales of mummies and mystery. Projects are being handed out and you are informed that you will be researching village life. Interesting? Yes, it is. Captivating? Possibly, but unlikely. By altering the task to engage students from the start—such as asking "What do you think made the biggest contribution to Ancient Egypt's society?"—we can engage our learners in critical thought and move away from a traditional fact-finding mission. Students feel empowerment when they can pick their own topic and they will research it with eagerness because they want to prove their topic is the most important. When we engage students and give them a sense of ownership, they naturally make deeper connections and more meaning in their learning. They start to think outside the box.

Now the magic starts, as students need to make connections, understand perspectives, make choices, and think critically about their task. They are making decisions and thinking about their topic prior to beginning their task. They are creating criteria about what is important as they follow through the process; they are supporting their opinions as they share their knowledge and complete the task. Through this process, students are placing value on their own understanding. The curriculum expectations have been met or exceeded, our students are intrinsically motivated, and they are finding deep connections that allow them to truly understand and conceptualize the topic of study.

A Driver's Manual: How to Make the Most of this Book

Like student-driven learning, this book will not follow a completely linear path. There is no one prescribed way to adopt the pedagogy that fosters student inquiry. Likely you will find yourself nodding your head often as you read the book. It may reinforce the practices you already support and give you new ideas that you can bring to your classroom. These nuggets, practical ideas along the path, brought us to our understanding and practice of student-driven learning. You might adopt all of these ideas as your own or, as we would advocate, you can choose to import the ones best-suited to your students, your classroom, and your school community.

SMALL HOPS

Look for the footprint icons in the margins. Small Hops are marked with one footprint; Medium-sized Drives with two; Big Journeys with three.

These small shifts tune up the classroom structures we use to set the tone and routines in the class. They expand current structures employed in the classroom and suggest ways to encourage student voice in shaping the classroom environment.

MEDIUM-SIZED DRIVES

Medium-sized Drives tackle rethinking and reorganizing how information is shared in the class. These ideas take a broad look at how we can engage students through exploring how their personal interests link to curriculum objectives.

BIG JOURNEYS

These big changes are meant to provoke thought about teaching and learning practices. They provide opportunities to foster student engagement and create a classroom where students learn their own way.

All suggestions—small, medium, and big—are presented through these elements:
  Destination: A quick glimpse of what you might expect as a learning outcome
  Shift: A description of how this idea shifts from a more traditional task to one that fosters student-driven learning

Sparks are not finite! As you and your students become more accustomed to the inquiry process, these hooks will naturally occur in the classroom environment.

  Spark: Critical-thinking questions and scenarios to engage and inspire discussion and thought among students
  Unfolding the Roadmap: Steps to take apart the idea
  Closure: A brief explanation of what you and your students might glean from the idea

Throughout the book you will encounter many of these ideas. They are not intended to be exclusively attached to the chapter they are found in, as the chapters themselves are deeper discussions about the elements of student-driven learning. Nor do we believe that one chapter or idea can be explored in isolation. The ideas are meant to connect, mesh together, and create a classroom that rumbles with its questions, creativity, and engagement.

We chose not number our ideas, as we have learned that nothing about natural inquiry is linear. It spreads and shrinks and takes new direction as students ask questions and home in on their own areas of interest.

In addition, text boxes explore examples and other topics that might further your appreciation of the trip.

Postcards from the Classroom: Throughout the book, you will find these boxes with anecdotes and examples from teachers on how activities and ideas have been implemented in their classrooms.

Detours: Along the way, we have included a few scenic detours. These detours explore topics in education that are relevant to student-driven learning. Detours are good spots to pause for a moment while you contemplate your teaching practice.

This book is not about rewriting the curriculum or writing individualized lessons and tasks for each of our students. It is our way of sharing how to create and involve students in the classroom so that they are empowered, engaged, and eager to learn. It is about creating lifelong learners who are ready for what the future might bring them. We will walk through the classroom experience, from that first intrepid September morning until the end of the year, taking Small Hops, Medium-sized Drives, and Big Journeys to bring our students back into the driver's seat and the excitement back into learning.

2

Taking a New Direction in Our Teaching Practice

> Study without desire spoils the memory, and it retains nothing that it takes in.
> — Leonardo da Vinci

Learning is not static. We are constantly learning. We adjust our understandings of social situations instantly as we read our peers' facial expressions. We change how we solve a tricky math question when we find out the answer is incorrect. We modify how to write a persuasive essay when our audience is not swayed to our viewpoint. While the big processes are occurring, we are also adapting our pen grip, saving files in new technologies, monitoring our body rhythms. In the process of acquiring this new knowledge, we never cease learning.

To learn means that we are modifying what we already know. It is the change that occurs when we acquire new knowledge, either because it extends what we already understand or because our current understanding has a flaw that needs to be solved. Learning is an active process. It is the process of acquiring this new knowledge that is learning. As we modify, rethink, and alter our current understanding, we are engaged in learning.

AVERAGE RETENTION RATES RELATED TO STUDENT ENGAGEMENT

Lecture	5%
What we read	10%
What we hear	20%
What we see	30%
What we see and hear	50%
What is discussed with others	70%
What we practice by doing	75%
What we experience personally	80%
What we teach others and use immediately	90%

Adapted from Ekwall (1974)

If we revert back to what we see as a traditional teaching model, in which information is being fed to our students, what are they learning? They are definitely engaged in learning, as learning is a constant and active process. But what are they actively learning? By lecture alone, they take in only 5%. What fills the other 95%?

We need to look to Ekwall's research to see how best to acquire a new understanding. To maximize the learning process we need to visualize, collaborate, communicate, and experiment with a concept. Our students need to play, think, wonder, and synthesize. We need to maximize their learning potential by building on their interests and natural curiosity. They need to play and experiment, to build on their knowledge and become the masters. To reach that 90% retention rate, they need to be driving their own learning and sharing it with others.

What Do We Want Our Students to Learn?

What is the end goal of formal education? Is it important that students can recite the structure of the feudal system, describe what synonyms are, or make food chains? These tidbits of information are important and, if the students are engaged, they can be very interesting. However, in the end, when students leave the education system and step out into the bigger world, what do they need to know? In our rapidly developing world, we can no longer cling to the idea that everyone must know the same things, that with a "blanket" education all students will emerge from the system with the same information and the same skills. It is impossible to fully prepare our students with all knowledge that will be required in their unknown future. Teaching our students to sit, listen, and systematically move through routines and information will not guarantee them a successful future.

What we can do, as educators, is teach our students how to learn; we can instill a sense of inquiry and wonder. Rather than memorizing facts, our students will need to know how to source information. Instead of reciting things learned by rote, they will need to know how to react to facial expressions. Students will need to know what to do with all kinds of information when they access it. They need to understand how to connect information, critically analyze it, get creative with it, and apply it to their new surroundings. They need to know how to learn actively.

What Are Our Roles?

As decrees our profession, the role of the teacher is never static. We used to be demonstrators, bearers of knowledge, dictators, social mediators, and even police officers, all wrapped up into one neat little package. As our classrooms have shifted to more engaged learning, increased use of digital technology, and collaborative structures, our role has also changed. Our students need different versions of "teacher" at different points in time. We continue to balance ourselves in various roles and juggle our interactions based on the needs of our students.

When asked *What is an effective teacher?* this is how our students responded:

- *The teacher would do a little bit of everything—a little working, a little playing, a little reading.*
- *Instead of doing regular math, make math into games.*
- *A teacher who makes it fun, not just work.*
- *Someone who makes real-life comparisons.*
- *Keeps you interested and engaged.*
- *Tells you about tests in advance.*
- *Does not give you praise when you don't deserve it.*
- *Someone who connects to the students.*
- *Funny, but knows when to be serious.*
- *They can be strict when they need to be, but not so strict that there is no fun.*

FACILITATORS

We are now the guides, facilitators, and meddlers. We need to help our students explore, wonder, ask questions, critically think, and ultimate learn important concepts in ways that promote active learning. We need to teach so that our students are engaged in and passionate about their learning, and we are guiding them to the end goal. As facilitators, we are listening to their ideas, collaboration, and goals. As meddlers we guide their process, model ideas, and push our students to think and explore ideas they might not have considered.

SKILL DEVELOPERS

We need ensure our students are prepared for the outside world. Certain basic skills are necessary, such as fluency with math facts and the structure of a sentence. More importantly, we also need to ensure our students have obtained the skills of learning, listening, and processing and adapting what they have absorbed. They need the skills of finding information, making connections, asking the right questions, and substantiating their answers.

ARTISTS

Our new role has us thinking outside of a textbook or procedural piece. We are not moving in a linear line. To facilitate and build our students' skills, we need to be divergent thinkers and consider which direction to push them in. We need to present options and think of problems and solutions that will extend their thinking. We need to think creatively about ways to reach our students and to inspire them to think creatively.

RESOURCERS

In our traditional teaching role of bearer of knowledge, we have been replaced. We are no longer expected to know all the information. The new bearer of knowledge is technology and our students have access to it. They can find information, match it to a visual, and possibly find a linking video to guide them step-by-step through a tricky concept. They do not need us to dictate facts or recite information; they can do that on their own in a few clicks. Their world is technology-based, and their future relies on their ability to find information quickly. Technology has not diminished our roles as teachers or the value of school. While students can access some information independently, curiosity needs fuel—that is the role of the educators. We also need to teach them how to sift through the information and to distinguish what information answers their questions, what information comes from a reliable source, and what information can be discarded.

COLLABORATORS

As we no longer deliver information, we are also learning with our students. We are guiding and facilitating, and also collaborating. We share directions or ideas to build on their ideas. We place them with an appropriate partner or push them in the direction of someone who will inspire them. We build a collaborative environment.

CRITICAL CHEERLEADERS

As our students learn, experiment, and try different solutions, we are part of their feedback. We need to guide them with a belief that they can do anything and then cheer them on when they achieve their goals. We need to build their creative confidence. We also need to step back and be realistic, set targets for them, and offer critical and obtainable feedback for growth.

DETOUR: PROFESSIONAL LEARNING COMMUNITIES

Endeavoring to do something different in our practice can be difficult if we feel we are alone in our decision to move away from tradition. While conversations in the staff room can give us some opportunity to share our experiences, these kinds of conversations are usually informal and may or may not be with people who are trying to do similar things.

In education, there has been a push to form professional learning communities (PLCs) at both grassroots and administrative levels. Richard DuFour, a leading figure in researching the efficacy of PLCs, describes a PLC as an ongoing process by which educators collaborate in inquiry and action research into best teaching and learning practices. The primary goal of any professional learning community in education is to improve student learning.

Sometimes these groups are formed within schools, across school boards, or through online communities. Online communities, with their global reach, can be especially enriching; you might be sharing and interacting with educators from all over the world.

Professional learning communities can provide

- Exposure to and development of new skills and capabilities
- Opportunities to share best practices with other teachers
- Increased communication and trust among teachers
- Possibilities to investigate different learning strategies
- Chances to develop new tools for teaching and assessment
- Reflection on evidence-based classroom research

"The growth of any craft depends on shared practice and honest dialogue among the people who do it. We grow by private trial and error, to be sure—but our willingness to try, and fail, as individuals is severely limited when we are not supported by a community that encourages such risks."
—Parker Palmer, *The Courage to Teach* (1988)

Small Hop: Teacher Check-In

DESTINATION

To get feedback from your students about how they see you as a teacher and how they feel in the classroom.

SHIFT

We have all been to teachers' college, we attend professional development, we read, we discuss with colleagues, we know the latest thoughts on pedagogy. What more do we need to consider when planning for our classroom? What about the voices of the students? How often do we seek their feedback on how they see the classroom environment and our role in the classroom? Done well, this is not an exercise in discomfort, but instead a worthwhile practice that helps us to know how we are viewed by our most-important evaluators.

SPARK

Explain to your students that, just as you provide them with a report card to give them feedback on their learning, it helps you to get feedback on how you are doing as their teacher. Be clear with students about the purpose of the exercise to ensure they are honest (and mature) with their feedback.

UNFOLDING THE ROADMAP

- Briefly explain the purpose of the exercise and what you are hoping to achieve. There are limitations to your powers as a teacher: some things are within your control (like how fast you talk), others are not (like extending recess for an hour).
- Create a short checklist for your students to complete. Ask questions that are simple, centred around the daily routines that matter. For example:

Think about things that are important to you in a teacher: Do they speak clearly? Do you understand their ideas? Do you feel comfortable asking them for help? Do you understand their feedback?

For younger children, the questions could be statements with a happy-face scale to measure their feelings.

- Read the checklists and look for trends.

CLOSURE

These surveys can be some of the most honest reflections you will receive about your teaching practice. Try to read what your students are expressing with an open mind and, after reading their input, choose one or two goals to work on. If you feel comfortable doing so, share these goals with the class. Ask for their help and feedback on how you can achieve the goals. Let them understand that for you, as for them, the work is always ongoing.

> **Consider keeping the surveys anonymous by option. I do—if a student wants me to know how they've responded, they can add their name.**

POSTCARD FROM THE CLASSROOM

I try to do a teacher check-in once a term. After the first one, the students are always eager for the next check-in. At first I was apprehensive and thought they might use the check-ins as revenge for a long homework activity. A few do approach the activity that way, but for the most part the students take this activity more seriously than anything I do with them. They feel quite honored that I actually ask their opinion about how I am doing, and they want to help me by giving me feedback. It is one of the easiest ways I can show them that I am interested in what they have to say. And, yes, every term their biggest issue is that I talk too much. So on that note, I will end this anecdote.

Make the Shift Step by Step

So where do we start? We have the curricular expectations, a classroom full of students, and an idea that they should be actively learning and fully engaged. Do we take the back seat, find the classroom sofa, and see what happens? No. There are two reasons for this: first, the classroom sofa probably contains more germs and living creatures than entire countries; secondly, because we are the teachers and we need to teach, guide, and facilitate how to think independently. We need bring out the richest, juiciest questions so that learning will be full of ideas and bring a deep understanding. Few students will leap into student-driven learning; some find it easier to follow instructions and safer to not think independently. We need to teach the students how to be in the driver's seat.

This can be a daunting task at the start of the year. Traditionally, our students come to us expecting us to tell them what to know. This is how school has worked for them in the past and they have an expectation that, once again, the teacher will tell them everything. For some students, having a teacher who does not profess to have all the answers can be confusing and, at times, discouraging. After all, teachers are supposed to know everything. Using the steps that follow will help unfold the idea in a manageable way. But be warned: once we have empowered our students, they will engage in their learning. They will come to us asking questions, eager to learn and to answer their own inquires.

1. Identify the Big Ideas

First, we need to know what to teach. What are the curricular goals for the year? What do we need to cover? Take a look at the expectations, overall and specific, and see if you can find ways to clump or sort them under themes appropriate to the unit. Just as we would with *backwards design*, we need to know what the students are expected to know before we begin.

2. Frontload to Complement Expectations

Our next step is to "frontload" information to our students so they have the context to ask meaningful questions in relation to what needs to be covered. We want to ensure that the expectations are met, so we need to provide information or resources that would lead our students in that direction. Understanding what needs to be taught helps us gather materials and supplies for frontloading that will guide our students in the direction of the expectations. For example, for a unit on the sun, many directions could be chosen and many questions could be asked. If we want our students to centre their questions around how the earth moves around the sun, we will put out a globe and books on the seasons; we can show a short online video about tilt or orbit. If we want our students to ask questions about the solar system, we will present different material for frontloading, such as planet books and pictures of stars, and possibly perform a gravity experiment. Frontloading provides us the opportunity to funnel the questions toward the end goal.

How much prior knowledge our students have on a topic determines how long and in-depth our frontloading needs to be. It is important to know that frontloading does not need to be a one-off lesson that moves quickly to the next point. Rather, it can be time where concepts are introduced and explored to create more meaningful questions. We can spend a lesson, a week, or more laying out the foundation for the questioning period. There are a variety of ways to introduce or frontload a new unit to students:

- Showing a video clip that gives a general overview
- Spreading out books, artifacts, and resources for the students to circulate and review
- Putting out the material to study
- Reading a story that relates to the topic
- Gathering articles on current events that relate to the topic and discussing them during class
- Beginning a story and then leaving it hanging at a critical point to prompt rich dialogue and questions
- Beginning with general lessons that cover the basics of the concept and provide vocabulary that will enrich the questioning

---

POSTCARD FROM THE CLASSROOM

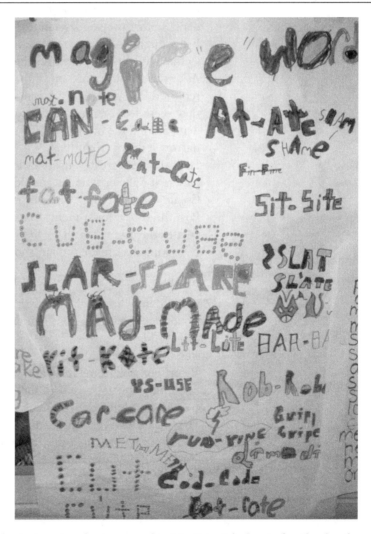

This brainstorming chart was used in Ms. Crippin's class to frontload and assess for prior knowledge on the concept of the magic *e*. Information was added as the term continued.

Medium-sized Drive: Open Frontloading

DESTINATION

To provide choice to our students' explorations and interpretations by allowing them to design their own task to demonstrate the expectation.

SHIFT

This step takes the traditional teacher's planning book and places it in the students' hands. It is an act of trust and respect on the teacher's part and an exciting window for students into the behind-the-scenes of the classroom.

SPARK

Post or print out the curriculum expectation that needs to be covered.

UNFOLDING THE ROADMAP

- Ask the students what they think of the expectation. Can they answer it?
- Deconstruct the teacher language: go through the expectations with the students so that they understand what they need to learn.
- Bring out a calendar and explain the timeline the expectation needs to follow so that students are fully informed and can make reasonable choices.
- Ask students to come up with a task or project that will demonstrate the required knowledge. What can they do to show they understand the task? If they seem lost or need guidance, you might bring in samples of projects students have done in the past. Or they can brainstorm what they like doing and narrow it down from there.
- Have the class create a list of criteria that all of their projects/tasks will need to adhere to. The criteria list should directly link back to the expectation.
- Create a class rubric that is broad enough to apply to all the different tasks. Post the rubric for students to use as an anchor and for a reference as you circulate and guide them back to the big ideas.
- Give students time; circulate, monitor, and keep meddling.

CLOSURE

Have students link their tasks back to the expectation. How do the tasks prove they understand it? Students can use the class rubric for self-assessment or each can share his/her task with the class. They can also justify which projects best linked back to the expectation, based on the criteria created earlier.

By properly planning the frontloading, we are guiding our students toward the curriculum expectations. Will there be unanticipated questions? Absolutely (we hope)! The goal of frontloading is to keep the questions along the general theme, the big idea. However, it is the questions we do not anticipate that will bring fresh and new ideas into our unit. It is these questions that will bring our students' interests and passions into the classroom and then transcend the classroom and enter their lives in an empowered and meaningful way.

3. Create Critical Questioners

In student-driven learning, learners need be critical questioners. They need to feel comfortable asking questions and, more importantly, they need to feel inspired to ask more questions once they get their first answer. Many of us ask questions not to gain new information, but to gain assurance that we are doing the right thing. Often a class conversation and activity can be derailed by questions like "Do I do it like this?" "What should I do next?" or, every teacher's most dreaded question, "Am I done?"

Questioning is a skill. Our students' questions will drive our unit, so it is important that we direct them toward richer questions that will prompt discussion rather than toward easily researched facts.

Asking questions follows this progression:

1. Understanding that questions begin with *who, what, when, where, why, how, if*. Depending on the word the question starts with, the context of the answer will be different. Our students need to understand that asking, "*Who* is the greatest leader in history?" will solicit a different response from "*What* was the greatest leader in history?" Our students need to understand that the words they choose affects how the question will be interpreted.

2. Asking deeper questions. By having our students categorize their questions, we are pushing them to think more critically about what they want to find out. Traditionally, we ask our students to make "big" questions using the starting words *how* and *why*. We can also push them to think about the kind of answer they are seeking: a quick one-word response or an answer that will extend into a conversation and variety of opinions?

3. Asking different questions. We need to model a balance of questions to ensure our students are looking at the topic from many different viewpoints. When looking at any topic, we want our students to think about these questions:

   - What is it like?
   - If we were to change it, what would we alter? Why?
   - How does it work?
   - Why is it like that?
   - How does it connect to our world?
   - How does it affect our world?
   - How do other people/cultures view it?
   - How do we influence it?

4. Sort the Questions into a Unit Structure

Once we have a bank of questions, we need to use them to guide the next few weeks of learning. "We" and "our" now represents both students and teacher. So where is *our* unit heading? What are *we* learning about, in what order, and when?

As a class, we need to take our questions and sort them into a logical order. We need to have a realistic timeline. Depending on the topic, as teachers we might need to guide students through this task. We can engage our students in organizing our unit in a variety of ways. They can work collaboratively, as a whole class, in small groups, or individually.

- Print the questions and have students cut them out to sort them into similar categories.
- Print the questions and use different-colored highlighters to put questions together.
- Students can select the major groups ahead of time and then sort the questions; as an alternative, they might look at all the questions, see what naturally works together, and then go from there.

This screenshot shows questions the students asked about the sun. We sorted our questions by placing them on the floor one at a time. As students read each question they determined if it fit with other questions or in its own category. As a class, they sorted the questions into five weeks, planning for the duration of the unit. The best part of engaging the students in the planning turned out to be that the students knew what we were learning throughout the process. I would quite often have a student or parent come with an artifact or sharing of knowledge because "We are going to study _____ this week."

Big Journey: Pushing for More Meaningful Questions

DESTINATION

To guide our students to ask deeper and more meaningful questions.

SHIFT

Teaching critical questioning skills is included in many curricular documents. Yet rarely is there emphasis placed on student accountability. Is the question meaningful? Is the question clear?

SPARK

Begin one day, or with a new unit, by asking the students to ask questions about the current topic. Have them write each question on its own sticky note or piece of paper. Discourage students from attaching their names, so that the questions can be looked at critically without emotional attachment.

UNFOLDING THE ROADMAP

- Have students read the pile of questions. Can they see a way to sort the questions? Ask: *Which questions will push our current learning and understanding?*

Which ones will help us think outside of the box? Which ones can we answer easily?

- Consider: when the question is driving the learning, is there a need for the student to ensure the question is worded correctly and is representing what they are wondering?
- See if the students can sort the questions into different groups. If they need assistance, you might post a few categories:

  Need-to-Know questions that seek out unknown information

  Private vs. Public questions that encourage the asker to consider if the information was useful/pertinent to all involved

  The-Sky-Is-Falling questions, or bizarre questions that really don't have an answer and only throw conversations off the tracks

  DIY (Do-It-Yourself) questions where the askers can easily figure out the answer themselves

  These categories, or the categories the students create, can stay up throughout the year to remind students how to seek out information they Need to Know without having to go through The Sky Falling.

- Find a place around the room to post the student questions; making them visible to you and the students will help ensure that you stay interested in finding out the answers.
- Have a pile of sticky notes ready for questions that will come as the unit progresses. Encourage students to add their questions as they come.
- What happens if students don't ask a question that is needed to guide the unit toward a major curriculum expectation? In this sticky situation, you can jump in and ask a question as well. You might choose to have core questions that address specific curricular goals. More often than not, the students will ask these questions themselves; if they don't, you might be able to slip your question into the mix. If names are assigned and individual tasks will be completed, then your ownership of the question allows you to share the information while modelling one way to respond.
- As the year evolves, this initial structure will be altered and extended. The students might identify certain questions that are factual in nature, with a clearly right or wrong answer. This discovery can create a new category—Right There questions—because we can find the answers right in a book or online. There may be other questions that invite us to share our opinion or perspective, helping to open up conversation. Groups of questions might be made to combine Right There information and our own thoughts.

CLOSURE

As the year develops, continue to ask questions and sort these questions. Throughout the sorting, we are also thinking critically about what we notice about our questions and how they drive the unit. For instance, students might notice that the combination questions yielded the best kinds of conversations.

Why were they built? (purpose/funtion)

What are the different types?

How does it help people? used?

What do we want to know about structures?

How are they built? (looks like, symmetry)

when were they first invented?

What are they made of?

Category	▽ 1	🍦 2	🍦 3	🍨 4
Make Sense	None - little	Some	About Structure – not specific to continent	All about structure and in continent
Detail	None - little	OK	Good 3/4	Lots → good words
Capitals + Periods	NO	A few	Most	All sentences
Neatness	Not	A bit	Most	Really

These two screenshots show how students were organizing a project on a particular structure. Once they decided on their structure, we sat as a class and brainstormed what we would like to know about that structure. This led into the rubric where the students created an open-ended assessment for their projects. Students were informed that the objective of this piece was to meet writing expectations.

Do the questions need an owner? Do our students put their names on their questions? This entirely depends on which direction we are taking in the unit. If we are looking at the questions as a collective and using them to guide the entire unit, then it is best if names are not assigned to the questions. As the unit develops, students are free to readjust their thinking, answer other interesting questions, release ownership of their questions. If the intention of the questions is to guide an independent project or to show a student's ability to pursue and find responses, then the student needs to put his/her name on the question.

Manage the Meddling

We have empowered, eager students awaiting the new unit. We have set up a unit for success by building our students' excitement and curiosity, so that these feelings are pushing them toward a deeper understanding. The students have a sense of what they are studying, they know the expectations they need to cover, and they have begun to ask some really solid questions about the new topic.

Now we need to help our students build their bank of knowledge. As we help them acquire the knowledge to meet the expectations, we are teaching them how to learn. Do we need to throw out our "oldies, but goodies" lessons? No. We are not re-creating the wheel, especially when we have tricks up our sleeves that we know work. Student-driven learning is about reshaping what we already know and need to do.

Big Journey: Making the Most of Magical Moments

DESTINATION

To maximize teaching moments for skill attainment.

SHIFT

Teachable moments have always been treasured in classrooms. By putting an intentional focus on creating teachable moments and attempting to maximize them, we are more attuned to the needs of our students, progressing at their rate and placing traditional skills lessons into a tangible context.

SPARK

A teachable moment is an unplanned time when we see the opportunity to offer guidance and insight. The spark might be a writing session when no one is writing a proper sentence. It could be a playground rumble when many are disgruntled and upset. It is a moment when we see the need to use a situation to address the involved individual, group, or whole class.

UNFOLDING THE ROADMAP

- Be aware of the needs of the students. Watch for times when students seek assistance or seem to be struggling.
- Gauge the damage. How many need assistance? Do we create a mini-group or address the whole class for a healthy review?
- Rather than focusing on a sequence of grammar or spelling-pattern lessons, use moments when the class, a group, or an individual struggles with a concept to review it.

- Be flexible with time and allow for teachable moments, even if they extend a lesson or project. When you maximize the teachable moment, the learning during the lesson or project is enhanced.
- Understand when the teachable moment has lost its momentum and head back to the task at hand.

CLOSURE

This moment can lead to further lessons, questions, or possibly a new direction in the current unit. Taking the time to follow a teachable moment brings authenticity to the classroom and the students, making our insight more valuable and easier to digest. It is also a stronger point of reference if students return to a similar area of difficulty at a later point.

POSTCARD FROM THE CLASSROOM

On a regular school day, our class was going through the motions of writing poetry. We were just beginning to discuss the process when a large excavator rolled up the street in plain view from our classroom window. To say the poetry lost some of its passion is an understatement. To make the most of this magical moment, I had the students grab clipboards and we went outside. We continued the poetry lesson using the excavator as our prompt. Some students chose to write about the birds or traffic. The topics had shifted from the original plan, but the product was much richer with the smells, texture, and inspiration that life presented before us.

3

Knowing Our Students

> Those of us who are in this world to educate—to care for—young children have a special calling: a calling that has very little to do with the collection of expensive possessions but has a lot to do with worth inside of heads and hearts.
>
> — Fred M. Rogers (*Mr. Rogers' Neighborhood*)

In all your years of teaching, have you ever taught two identical children? Children who act the same and think the same? It is true that, after many years in the classroom, within the first few days of the year we can identify the energetic ones, the outspoken ones, the quiet ones, the imaginative ones, the reluctant ones, the anxious ones, the wild ones, the rude ones, the "oh my god, how will I survive a year with you" ones…and the list goes on. But those characteristics are generalizations—as the year progresses, every child will eventually play every role mentioned. The nature of different people can be similar but the individual essence of each person is unique. How each of us perceives information and acts on our thoughts is very different. What matters to us is different. Our perception of our world is different. We are all individuals.

If we are not careful as teachers, we tend to view our students through the stereotypes attached to them. The labels on the individualized student reports, the stories from the staff room, the opinions of their peers, the run-in you had with the rambunctious student two years ago at recess—these experiences influence how we perceive the students in our classroom. If we never take the time to claim each of our students as unique and powerful players in the classroom, we do ourselves, and them, an incredible disservice.

The beginning of the school year is chaotic: you are establishing the tone in the classroom, trying to get preliminary assessments completed, dealing with overly interested (or completely uninterested) parents, trying to get started with all the curricular goals, and, if you are like me, shaking off your summer melancholy. It is not difficult at this time to miss the most important opportunity as an educator—the chance to develop an emotional bond with your students.

Despite how much we analyze, categorize, and assess our students, research shows that nothing amounts to more improvement in a student than the emotional bond that student has with his or her teacher. From our first greeting each morning to the end of the day goodbye, we have an opportunity to connect with each of our students.

DETOUR: RELATIONAL TEACHING

In 2008, a meta-study (directed by Melbourne Graduate School of Education's Professor John Hattie) of 80 million students from around the world found "positive teacher–student interaction" to be the single most important factor in better education outcomes. The importance of developing a positive relationship with your students surpasses all else in its influence to encourage student success. As teachers we see daily what happens when we make a priority of building relationships with our students.

Relational teaching is the term for personally engaging with the students, having students personally engage with each other, and creating a classroom community in which students are engaged and supportive.

To promote relational teaching:

- Learn about each student's interests and talents
- Identify a special need of each student, and meet it
- Find and share a common interest
- Be prepared to accept a few grumpy moments or exchanges with a student
- Maintain clear and valued standards in the classroom
- Provide time for students to share personal experiences
- Every once in a while, make an exception
- Share personal stories that reveal moments of vulnerability or uncertainty
- Celebrate any commonalities
- Let students know that you want them to be successful, and be persistent in your efforts to help them find success

Adapted from Reichart (2010)

Get to Know the Individual

Identify the Unique

Each year, we welcome anywhere from 20 to 30 strangers into our classroom. They are eager, curious, and every bit as nervous and excited about what the year holds as we are. Understanding these individuals and their individual strengths is essential to the class dynamic and individual relationships.

At each encounter we have with our students, individually or as a group, we are reading them. And they are reading us. It is an unwritten law to navigate around the other people around you. It seems so simple but is so complex. Knowing our students, who they really are from their perspective and from our perspective, will help shape the classroom and the year.

> When asked, this is how students responded to *What do you want your teachers to know about you?*
>
> - *What sports I play*
> - *What we do out of school*
> - *That we are cool*
> - *How hard we work*
> - *Who our friends are*
> - *Our strengths and weaknesses so they can adapt their teaching*
> - *What is going on in our community, understanding if the work is not done*

From their perspective, we need to know the following:

- *What are our students passionate about?* Passions are what drive and motivate us. By understanding and remembering our students' passions, we can help create a context of tasks they might like, units will that excite them, and topics to bring up to help them make connections. If we know that Stephanie loves dinosaurs and struggles when writing, we can use her passion as a topic to produce more creative writing.
- *What shuts our students down?* Just as we "bank" what our students are passionate about, we must remember and understand what causes them anxiety or stress. We are going to encounter students who may not be able to deal with certain topics due to their past experiences; our common sense tells us to tread lightly on topics, such as death, when a student has recently struggled with experience of them. Being prepared with this information as early as possible helps us create a classroom that feels safe.
- *What discourages our students?* We need to know where our students are going to be successful. But at the same time, part of being successful is overcoming obstacles. Identifying and understanding why certain challenges are obstacles will help us prepare our students to be successful. If we have weak readers and we choose to provide a task that is entirely written, we need to modify the wording and supplement the written instructions with visuals or oral instructions prior to beginning.
- *What do students see as their next steps?* Our students have a strong understanding of what they want to know and learn. They compare themselves to others. Even in a Kindergarten class, the children can identify the neatest printer or the ones who can read smoothly. Older students have created, met, and rewritten goals before. They have a sense of what they feel comfortable with and what areas they would like to work on. Having students share with us their goals or next steps for the school year or week ahead helps us gain a better understanding of how they see themselves in their learning and what they are most self-conscious about.

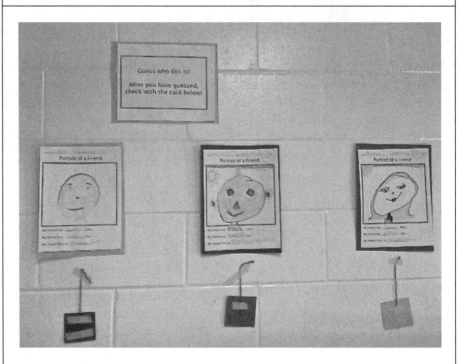

In Christina Morgan-Poort's Grade 1/2 split, the students thought of facts that described them. These facts were hung on the wall with their self-portraits and students had to guess who each person was. This kind of introductory activity is a fun, hands-on way for students to learn about each other, independently and throughout the day. It also allows each student to claim the unique facts that will make him or her different from everyone else.

Identify Strengths

As teachers, we have a desire to quickly assess where students are lacking, either individually or as a whole, and we make it our job to "fix" this problem. Certain areas we can predict. We know that very young students are going to struggle with working in groups, especially when some are still engaged in parallel play. We know the academic knowledge that most students will need at the age level we teach, be it making friends, mental math, the concept of fractions, or forming a persuasive essay. This has been our role for centuries. We have been the fixers: we prepare our students for the next step. People put considerable importance on a teacher's ability to impart knowledge.

We need to shift our students from only relying on us to learn to also taking learning into their own hands and sharing their learning with their peers. Nurturing our students' strengths and finding ways to use those strengths to collaborate with peers or further their own learning is also teaching a life skill. Our first step to building on our students' strengths is to gain a better understanding of them as individuals.

From our perspective, we need to know the following:

- *How do our students interact with others?* Understanding our students' individual social strengths and areas for improvement and development will be key to helping our students progress throughout the year. The classroom is a social experience and we need to know how each student copes with and thrives in this dynamic.

- *How does each student work best?* Do they perform better individually or in groups? Do they need a space on their own in a quiet focused area to concentrate or do they thrive with music and being in the centre of the room?
- *What assets do they bring?* Identifying our students' strengths helps us prepare them to be leaders in those areas. They can use these strengths for assisting others, modelling tasks. and identifying what the next steps are. We also need to know where the ceiling is for their strengths, how far can we nudge our students before they reach the point of frustration.
- *How do they respond to different experiences: e.g., with happiness, frustration, disappointment?* The school year is full of change and healthy challenge. What will be our students' reactions during these pivotal moments? How do they share their excitement and how do they cope with less-positive situations? Being able to predict or know a student's reaction helps prepare us. It also provides a window into how a student might be feeling.
- *What areas do we see as work in progress?* Our goal is still to help our students grow to their potential; that means we need to assess what our students' next steps are, just as they learn to.

How do we gain this information? It is fine to say that we need to learn all of these facts but, if we have 30 students swinging in 30 different directions with multiple learning styles, abilities, strengths, areas of improvement, and personalities, how do we gather needed individual information on each student?

Small Hop: Beginning-of-the-Year Letter Home

DESTINATION

To collect student information from home and from the students themselves.

SHIFT

While collecting individual data is important for starting the year, such information is difficult to obtain when we are establishing many new routines. By sending a letter home that requests this information, we are inviting our parents and students to be partners in their learning. We are validating parents' knowledge of their children and the voices of our students. We are also laying a foundation for a collaborative relationship and outlining our teaching philosophies.

SPARK

As a lure to task completion, link parents' participation to a curriculum night or interview night where the details parents and students provide will be discussed. This link will establish the importance of their dialogue, as well as signalling greater significance for the task.

UNFOLDING THE ROADMAP

- Send home a letter to outline the task, discussing why it is important and how you will use this information.
- Encourage parents and children to work together to complete the task, including their different perspectives.

- In the questionnaire, include a range of activities or questions that captures both the child's social/emotional abilities and the academic issues.
- You might choose to have older students write their own letters or complete the questionnaire in class, where they can feel the autonomy of not needing parent feedback. You could also send home an additional letter for parents to complete with or without the student.
- Here is a sample letter, addressed to the student:

Dear Samuel,

I am thrilled to be learning with you this year. A big part of starting off this adventure together is having a better understanding of each other. Included with this letter is a list of activities that I hope you will complete with your family. Please sit down and talk about what activities you love, which activities you feel comfortable with, and which ones you would like to get better at.

I want to ensure that that the curriculum and learning activities this year are meaningful to you. By having a better understanding of what you enjoy and what you do not like, I will get a sense of what motivates you and what you see as goals for the year. Although I cannot promise to incorporate all of your favorite activities, this list will help me tailor assignments and activities to incorporate your interests.

When you have completed the checklist, please select the top four things that you feel I should know about you. These four items can be things that you enjoy or would like to work on.

On Monday, I will share my list of activities and my top four items with you so that you have a better sense of what learning with me will be like. On September 28, the school is hosting a settling-in interview and you and your parents are invited to discuss the transition into our classroom. On this night, we will also take a moment to discuss your list of top four items.

Please let me know if you have any questions or concerns.

Sincerely,

POSTCARD FROM THE CLASSROOM

Please place a checkmark in the box you feel most represents you	I love this	I feel comfortable with this	I would like to work on this
Playing with friends	☐	☐	☐
Reading stories	☐	☐	☐
Working all by myself	☐	☐	☐
Meeting new friends	☐	☐	☐
Listening to stories	☐	☐	☐
Following rules	☐	☐	☐
Helping others	☐	☐	☐
Sharing with others	☐	☐	☐
Talking about stories	☐	☐	☐
Solving problems	☐	☐	☐
Tidying up	☐	☐	☐
Working with others	☐	☐	☐
Sharing my ideas with the class	☐	☐	☐

This sample shows a possible task sheet for a younger primary student. The expectations are intentionally mixed up (i.e., social skills are not grouped together; reading skills are not grouped together), requiring student and parents to read each one and not just follow a theme.

POSTCARD FROM THE CLASSROOM

I begin every year by giving each student a letter I've written to the class. In my letter, I talk about my summer, my personal interests, my family, and anything else I think they might be curious about. After finishing my letter, I ask them to write me a letter back. If they retort that they can't think of anything, I tell them to look at my letter and find some ideas. These letters help me learn about my students' likes and dislikes (yes, some do include "letter writing" in their dislikes), and the other nuances that make them who they are. They provide me with a starting point for how I can connect with each of my students. It is a simple but powerful way to begin the year—by showing my students that I care to know who they are.

> When I am not teaching, my hobbies include running, bicycling, swimming, hiking, gardening, reading, cooking (and eating) and cartooning. My favorite things to eat are pizza (ham and pineapple) and candy. I am usually a happy person, but there are a few things that drive me nuts: getting my socks wet (when my feet are in them), mean people, throwing away things that can be reused, and hard licorice.
>
> Flashback to me in Grade 5…my favorite author was Gordon Korman. My favorite subjects in school were art, drama, and language. When I was in Grade 5, I thought I would be a photographer, a teacher, or a cartoonist. So here I am, a teacher who cartoons and takes pictures.

CLOSURE

By sending this task home with students, we create a stronger bond between school and family. Parents feel validated and students begin to discover the power of their voice. This document also acts as one of our first formal pieces of assessment for learning (see page 104). We can use this data to determine the interests of our students and the areas they feel they need work on. We can use it to match students with similar interests or areas for improvement, or we can use it to pair up students with differing abilities for collaboration.

Intelligence in Education

The idea of intelligence is critical in student-driven learning. Some educators feel that those who excel in a student-driven learning model are those who are highly intelligent. And often, in using the term "intelligence," they are referring to students who do consistently well in formal evaluations. We believe differently:

intelligence is expressed in many forms and, unlike traditional education, student-driven learning offers a framework that will allow for all children to find success within the regular program.

Cognitive science outlines that there is more than one type of intelligence. And there are many theories on various types of intelligence. This makes sense. If only one type of intelligence was needed, the world would be linear and every failure would be explained with the same response: "Those who fail went off the linear path." Thankfully our ways of thinking are not linear. We meet individuals who excel in academics but not in life, or ones who succeed in life but failed in school. We meet individuals who can answer complex algorithms yet struggle with practical life decisions and functionality. We meet individuals who excel in one discipline but struggle in another. Happily, there is no one path in learning that is suited to all—how would we ever be inspired to think deeply if we all moved along the same path?

The theories on intelligence have shaped and reshaped our teaching. Howard Gardner changed our perception of what it means to be intelligent. He compiled nine intelligences—naturalist, musical, logical-mathematical, existential, interpersonal, bodily-kinesthetic, linguistic, intrapersonal, and spatial—to enhance the various lenses through which we look at our students. Theories and experiments on the differences between reasoning in the right-brain and left-brain have also helped expand our notion of what intelligence requires; i.e., both linear and random thought processes. This century has also focused the spotlight on practical knowledge and an understanding how to interact with the world around us.

What is the essence of all of these theories?

- Everyone has the ability to foster his or her own intelligence.
- People have various strengths. There is no single way to be intelligent.
- We all learn differently, depending on where our strengths or intelligences lie.
- As teachers, we cannot consistently teach one way and catch the interest of all of our students.
- Our students will develop at different rates and in different ways because of their different strengths.

A Shift in What We Know about Intelligence

Which column resonates with something you might have heard before?

• I cannot do that.	• That looks like a challenge.
• The test proves that you do not know your math.	• You need to practice your recall of math facts to improve on the harder questions.
• Your intelligence is a part of you that you cannot change.	• You can learn new things and grow your intelligence.
• I am smart because I was awarded the gold star.	• I feel smart when I figure out something tricky.

The first column is typical of a mindset in which intelligence is viewed as fixed. A person uttering these lines would believe that intelligence is a born right and that we have a finite capability. The second column represents intelligence as growth; as something we can foster and develop; as something obtainable.

To delve further into how one's perception of intelligence shapes learning, read Carol Dweck's book *Mindset*.

For our students to develop to their full potential, we need to foster their growth intelligence. We need to push them into believing in themselves and knowing that they can accomplish what they would like. When our students are engaged, they can move mountains. We want to make sure that they visibly see their growth so that they continue to foster it themselves. By fostering our students' growth intelligence we are claiming our students and showing them that we believe in them.

INTELLIGENCE THAT MOVES FORWARD

We believe that, in our present world and in our students' future, our students will need to connect globally, create opportunities, and think beyond the expected. They will need the types of intelligence that a computer cannot hold for them. While a strong knowledge base and skill set are undeniable elements of an intelligent individual, we need to recognize and value intelligences that cannot be acquired through rote learning or memorization.

EMOTIONAL INTELLIGENCE

Emotional intelligence is the ability to respond intelligently to life situations. As our students move forward, they will need a sense of who they are emotionally. Emotional intelligence is based on how we perceive ourselves as individuals. It is the perspective we have of ourselves within this crazy world. With emotional intelligence, we want to foster

- Confidence: a feeling of success over the unknown, an ability to see the positive prior to the negative
- Curiosity: the wonder and desire to find out about things
- Resilience: the determination to continue when obstacles are presented
- Self-Control: the ability to use inner power to regulate actions
- Relatedness: the ability to interact with others with the sense of being understood
- Communication: the desire to share information with others
- Cooperation: the ability to balance one's own needs with those of others

In a large way, emotional intelligence shapes our abilities. Think of it this way… Who loves math? Answer: The students who feel confident and successful at it. Who loves art? Answer: The students who feel confident and successful at it. Who loves writing stories? Answer: The students who feel confident and successful at it. Positive emotional connection shapes our learning. When they have a positive association with learning, our students feel like they can excel, drive to solve problems, and arrive upon results that demonstrate their confidence. By fostering our students' emotional intelligence, we are setting them up for success both in academic tasks and in life.

SOCIAL INTELLIGENCE

Social intelligence is, in one word, empathy. The umbrella of empathy covers all social interactions. Our world is becoming more global. A huge part of participating successfully in our world is understanding how to be empathetic. Our students need to be empathetic to

- Interpret/read other's emotions
- Understand perspective as an individual point of view; understand how perspective changes with each individual
- Respond appropriately in different situations and with different people

As a primary teacher, I am asked by parents, "When do you introduce chapter books?" or I hear students proudly exclaim, "I am reading chapter books." There seems to be a fixation on reading the chapter book as a milestone for young students; however, young children need to be able to read more than chapter books to succeed. They have to know how to read visual cues to interpret social situations. Many text forms support this kind of development: picture books, graphic books, etc. The key is to balance the types of texts that students read so they can do more than race from picture book to chapter book.

- Think with the perspective of the larger social world and the dynamics of the various people in it

Our classroom is the ultimate social setting and the place where our students interact with each other. For some of our students, this is their only opportunity to connect with others on a regular basis. For all of our students, the classroom is an important space to develop their emotional intelligence. Our students' daily interactions teach them how to respond to each other; how to navigate their own path in a busy place, optimizing the individuals around them; and how to maximize their social interactions to suit their needs. If we shift to a student-driven classroom, a student's peers in the classroom also act as valuable tools. They can

- Push a thought to a deeper level
- Change the direction of thinking by asking a question
- Offer suggestions
- Provide structured or critical feedback
- Be an emotional support

REASONING INTELLIGENCE

Like social intelligence, reasoning is an umbrella. It involves all the creative and critical thought processes one might experience while thinking. If our emotional intelligence is how we develop our inner self and our social intelligence is how we foster our relationships and interactions with others, then reasoning encompasses the rest. When reasoning, we are

- Solving problems
- Stepping "outside the box" by thinking laterally/creatively so that various ideas are presented
- Analyzing and judging our ideas to select the best one
- Critically thinking; pushing ourselves to a deeper level of understanding

To foster our students' reasoning intelligence in the classroom, we can

- Guide them through various processes of solving problems so that they can decide what works for them
- Provide them the tools they will need, which might include writing, number sense, logic, typing, summarizing information, etc.
- Challenge them to think outside their usual parameters to extend their ideas
- Be their critical cheerleader, who positively supports them, but also provides constructive feedback to move them forward

Our different types of intelligences—emotional, social, and reasoning—are intertwined. We act with all.

Skill	Emotional Intelligence	Reasoning Intelligence	Social Intelligence
Collaborating	Using the knowledge gained in the collaborative setting to further individual understandings.	Listening to ideas and formulating their own ideas; thinking through the problem.	Being able to work in a group; understanding the feelings of others and how that influences the learning.

Creating	Feeling free to create and be creative, confident in the ability to produce.	Using the tools needed and the process of planning to produce creatively.	Sharing resources and ideas with others; offering feedback and constructively using feedback offered.
Communicating	Expressing a desire to share ideas in a constructive manner.	Understanding the tools and the process of sharing information.	Reading the emotions of others; using this to gauge how to frame new information.

We shift to a growth mindset as we think of our students, where they are and where they want to be, realizing they have almost limitless potential.

Big Journey: Emotional Check-Ins

DESTINATION

To gather data on how our students are coping in the classroom, encompassing their emotional, social, and reasoning intelligence.

SHIFT

Taking a moment to identify who our students are as individuals is often a big assignment: students share their experiences, family trees are drawn, photos are pasted on Bristol board, and posters emerge around the classroom. Taking time to deeply investigate who our students are can result in valuable lessons. We can complement these activities with periodic quick check-ins that are webbed into our regular routines, offering our students a chance to voice their emotions about themselves, the social classroom, or their progress while reasoning.

SPARK

Begin the year by talking about how the way we feel links to how we learn. When we are nervous, tired, sad, angry, stressed, etc., all these emotions directly affect how we learn. Simply put, our brain will not work as well if we are not feeling well.

UNFOLDING THE ROADMAP

- Using a simple graphing program for attendance, have each student sign into class by sharing a personal response. This attendance strategy can be used to finish or start a new unit, or when you sense turmoil coming. The posted question might be "How do you feel about starting a new unit today?" with a list of drop-down options in a range covering *Excited, Good, Okay, Nervous, Sad.* The interactive whiteboard makes setting this up very manageable.
- Create a mailbox or a place where students feel free to write their concerns, ideas, or just thoughts. This might extend to a Mailperson job of delivering letters all over the school to siblings, the principal, etc. Everything from "I miss you" to "We need a better play structure" can be voiced.
- At the end of the day, ask your students to give you a quick rating for the day. Be forewarned: if you stop the students who are brave enough to give a low

rating, you might not get honesty next time. Make a mental note of the low rating and, if need be, privately touch base with the student the following day.

- Create a class tag cloud (e.g., Wordle at www.wordle.com) where students can add an adjective to describe their feelings about an event or unit. When a tag cloud is created at the start of a unit, it can be great for reflection as the unit or activity progresses.
- Set up a media collection (e.g., VoiceThread at www.voicethread.com) where students can share their thoughts and ideas in a video-diary format.
- Read facial cues. Take time to acknowledge an upset student or one who looks frustrated. If possible, ask other students to read their peer's face and see if they can help solve the problem.
- Ask for thumbs-up/thumbs-down when you want to do a quick check-in for understanding or mood.
- With younger children, make sure you have pictures of different facial expressions available. To check in on students' frame of mind, have them line up behind the expression that coordinates with their mood.
- Create class value lines (with bodies or names on sticky notes): ask students to respond to a statement; e.g., *I really enjoyed reading our class novel aloud.* They stand or "stick" themselves to a spot on the value line.
- Sit down. Find time to sit and talk to your students. Focus on them, not on lesson objectives or catch-up items.

CLOSURE

Quick emotional check-ins not only offer our students a voice beginning, during, and at the end of our studies, but also allow us a chance to connect to our students on a more regular basis. We can use this information to feed into the classroom dynamic.

POSTCARD FROM THE CLASSROOM

A few weeks into the school year, I always get my students to jot down some ideas of things that bug them. They love it—a chance to complain. These ideas, though, provide the context for some great discussions around what they care about. These charts give me insight into how they are feeling at a particular moment, and they also are a rich source for potential research topics.

Addressing Learning Diversity

In every classroom exists a wide range of learning diversities. We know there is no one-size-fits-all activity that works for a classroom teacher. Every lesson, every unit, even every minute classroom interaction needs to be tweaked to reach different students.

Some students enter the classroom with road maps that outline their learning needs, educational plans that employ a number of strategies to be used to help the learner connect with the curriculum and their classmates. More often than not, the strategies provided for individuals are ones that benefit the whole class. These strategies naturally meld with a program that fosters student interests and abilities.

Learning strategies supported by student-driven learning:

- Increased student engagement
- Making connections between content and prior knowledge
- Using different types of literacy (text, visual, Web, etc.)
- Minimizing excess information and focusing on big ideas; i.e., focus on concepts rather than disparate facts
- Hands-on learning
- Promoting active reasoning

Student-driven learning is more activity-driven than conventional teaching perspectives and it allows for exploration. When students are able to explore a concept or idea, either through active manipulation or active reasoning, they are more likely to retain the information. Research has indicated that using a discovery approach to learning, as opposed to direct instruction, can help students remember information for longer periods of time.

An Environment *For* the Students

One critical aspect of engaging and knowing your students is creating a classroom that reflects their interests and allows for independent exploration.

Each year the catalogues seem to come thicker, with new ideas, posters, themes, and gadgets for the classroom. With a click of a button, you can purchase an entire classroom, complete with laminated clocks, seasons charts, little bears holding the title of classroom jobs, and apple-adorned welcome signs. It is possible to create a cozy, glossy, and welcoming classroom using these resources. Yet we do not, or cannot, all prescribe to these kinds of classrooms. There are obvious reasons: the cost, the amount of labor, the teetering stools required to staple the seasons charts into the corners of the room. But for most of us, the reasons extend beyond financial and workplace hazards. We want our students to bring their own mark to the classroom. If our students walk into a room that is "done," what is there left for them to do? How can they feel ownership of their learning space if the space itself is complete on the first day of school?

In his JK/SK class, Mr. V. uses picture cues to show the schedule for the day. Students have a visual image from their own classroom to remind them what was happening on any given day.

Arrange Classroom Resources

As our year starts, it is the time when we set our atmosphere and prepare our students to begin making their own decisions. We begin to hand over the responsibility prior to setting up the classroom. We need to think about building a classroom that both is accessible and includes our students in the process.

Small Hop: Classroom Design

DESTINATION

To consider how the physical set-up of a classroom can encourage student-driven learning.

SHIFT

In a classroom where all the resources are neatly stored behind the teacher's desk or in a locked closet, students are not taught to exercise independence or restraint. In a classroom that engages students in their own learning process, all parts of the classroom, materials, and tools need to be accessible to the students. We want our students to be able to reach the tools they need to learn. And we want our students to have the comfort and confidence to access these tools without constantly seeking permission.

SPARK

Prior to the start of the year, make a quick map of where you have placed resources in the classroom. Ask yourself if these resources (especially those that are used daily or often) are in eyesight of the children.

UNFOLDING THE ROADMAP

- Consider the placement of pencils, erasers, markers, pencil crayons, glue, and general classroom supplies. If students are coming from a space where these items were guarded, they may initially, shocked by the free access, consume or waste more general supplies than the budget allots. In this situation, students can brainstorm ways to stop the supply crisis. One classroom job might be Supply Manager, so there is a check point. They can also budget the supplies so that new pencils and other tools are released on a monthly schedule.

- If your classroom has an interactive whiteboard, it needs to be at a level that all students can access. It needs to be low enough so that the students can reach most of it, but high enough so that the board can be seen from the various desks in the room. If you aren't able to install it according your students' height, purchase a sturdy stool that will "live" under the whiteboard and allow students to reach it.
- The classroom schedule must be posted in a clear and kid-friendly manner. Ideally the students will participate in changing the daily class schedule.
- Any resource texts should be readily available to all the students. Aesthetically, well-thumbed reference books might look better spine-out on a high shelf; however, it is important to have these resources within arm's reach. Dictionaries, thesauruses, math reference books, atlases, and whatever else you might refer to during a daily class should have a highly visible spot within your classroom. Having a dictionary on a table, rather than buried on a shelf, encourages students to use it frequently.
- Games and tools should be sorted and stored at an accessible level. Many of our math or language supplies come out at specific times of the year; e.g., manipulative clocks during the measurement unit. If you theme shelving units to subject or create an organizational system that is easy for the students to decode, you enable them to find tools easily without seeking assistance. For instance, keeping all math supplies together on one shelf allows students to confidently find what they need.

CLOSURE

At the start of the year, you will need to be more mindful of ensuring that students find the resources for themselves. As well, reinforcing routines about organization of resources and use of the resources will help ensure that the classroom is neat and that students are responsible for their materials. Once these routines are in place, it feels wonderful when students stop following you around the classroom, parroting, "I need markers," "I need pencils," "I need an eraser."

POSTCARD FROM THE CLASSROOM

Going through old resources that had been in my classroom through several generations of teachers, I found a dusty set of dictionaries. I prepared to recycle the monsters when one student stopped me. He couldn't believe that there was a dictionary so big it had to be kept in three books. The dictionary set never made it to the recycling bin. Instead, the class decided that the "Super Dictionary"—all three volumes—should be placed on a table, out in the open, where they could use it to check their spelling and find possible spelling words. There was much prestige around using the Super Dictionary, and it became a well-thumbed and much-loved emblem of our classroom.

Share the Responsibility

Providing our students with "jobs" or tasks, either on a rotational cycle or as they come up, is a philosophy that many teachers support. We empower our students by asking them to deliver a message, take attendance or hand out notebooks. We are teaching them to be responsible by trusting them with responsibilities that they see are necessary.

Small Hop: Collaborative Job Board

DESTINATION

To empower our students by creating a collaborative classroom job board.

SHIFT

Classrooms are run with the help of eager students who want to assist. We either catch them as a job comes up or select a few jobs that they can handle for the start of the year. Rather than assigning classroom jobs, invite students to decide how they can participate in helping the classroom. What do they see that they can do?

SPARK

Begin with chaos. Hold up an envelope and ask, "Can someone really responsible help me? This envelope is very important and needs to be delivered." Watch as your students frantically wave their hands in the air and scramble toward you, eager to be selected as the sole responsible student.

POSTCARD FROM THE CLASSROOM

This is a job board from Ms. Ryder's Grade 4 classroom. The students designed the jobs and the name tags. The board is at a level that students can access so they can manage it. At the start of every week, the students draw sticks to choose their job for the week. There is quite a clamor as each student works to get his/her favorite job and, as a result, each takes the role seriously.

- Gather the students and ask, "How can we make this fair?" Ensure that they understand that they are all responsible and there needs to be a way that everyone can help out. This is also a wonderful time to add a dramatic flair, talking about how there are many jobs or tasks that could use responsible students.
- Have the students begin by brainstorming tasks they would complete daily; e.g., sharpening pencils, tucking in chairs. Record these ideas on a mind map or list.
- Extend the list by asking what else could be done in the classroom. Have students brainstorm ideas, such as Line Leader, Board Eraser, Attendance Monitor. If there is a job that will be needed later in the year but is forgotten at this point, join the conversation and add it or hint at it.
- Decide on the number of jobs needed. Ask students, "If we have 24 students, how many jobs do we need? Should we think of eight and rotate each week? Or do we have 12 jobs we can rotate every other week? How should we rotate to make it fair to everyone?"
- From the sharing, create a board of jobs and a rotation cycle. The students might need to vote if there are more jobs than needed.

CLOSURE

Have students write the titles of the jobs and possible descriptions. This is also an opportunity for students to extend their vocabulary; e.g., "What title can we create that would match the job of handing out supplies? Supply Manager." Students can create a bulletin board with the job titles, descriptions, and a class list to check off names as they complete a job, to ensure that the same job is not repeatedly done by the same student.

4

Fueling the Learning Spark

Study without desire spoils the memory, and it retains nothing that it takes in.
— Leonardo da Vinci

Turn on the TV or flip through a book and it is easy to find examples of unmotivated students: Bart Simpson, his eyes glazed over as the teacher speaks; Charlie Brown listening to the tinned gibberish of the teacher; Calvin plotting mass destruction rather than completing his math test. These characters are parodies of students we know from our own teaching. No teacher is without his or her story of the student who drifted off in class. We can blame lack of breakfast, too much activity at recess, a late night watching TV…or we can simply acknowledge that sometimes our classrooms are not always the most riveting places for our students' attention.

When I first began teaching, I tried to make every moment a magical one. I was determined to banish any hint of boredom or drudgery from my curriculum. The end result: a classroom of overexcited Grade 3 students and a very tired teacher. As educators, we all understand that there needs to be a balance between calm and chaos in our classroom and that students will learn and flourish at different points in this balancing act.

There is no one secret to engaging all of our students. Our learners come with a kaleidoscope of different personalities and abilities. What might spark one student's interest could be a tedious task for another. We cannot expect our students to show equal levels of engagement with the same task or subject matter. Simply put, it is easy for students to get bored if they do not see the personal value in the task. Student-driven learning attempts to circumvent the waning interest of our students and provide a classroom where students can become engaged with their learning process.

Engagement and Motivation in the Classroom

"Just do it." This well-known slogan is famous for its apparent ability to motivate. As a society, we are obsessed with the idea of motivation. A quick Google search reveals that more than 214 million sites have *motivation* as a key word. We talk about motivation in reference to almost any discipline. In education, entire texts are devoted to how we can foster motivation in our classroom. Understanding what motivates us and how we can motivate others has become a massive industry in education.

"X needs to show motivation to _____." Fill in the blanks and you have a statement that is said, written, and included in assessments in classrooms around the world. But how often do we actually help our students create a plan to show this motivation? And more importantly, are we reflecting on the reasons why X is lacking in motivation? We know that our students will show greater interest when they see the personal value in a task. Interest continues to increase when the task is one that the students have selected themselves.

We know, when it comes to lifelong learning, passion always beats brains. If we can discover what interests our students and help foster these interests within our teaching, we will be able to create a learning environment that engages our students more readily.

Medium-sized Drive: An Interest Inventory

DESTINATION

Have all students complete an interest inventory when the class begins a new year, month, task, unit, or project. Used for almost any purpose, an interest inventory allows students to reflect on areas of personal interest. It can also provide the teacher meaningful feedback for moving forward with a class project or activity.

SHIFT

In a traditional classroom, students are assigned an "interest" by teachers, by peers, or because they do not know enough about a topic or task to care. By taking time to survey students about their interests at the start of an activity, teachers encourage students to reflect on their likes/dislikes and give these opinions credibility in the learning process.

SPARK

Gather a list of words, visuals, or objects related to the topic. Ask students to pick one. As they respond, record their thoughts as a whole class or as individuals.

UNFOLDING THE ROADMAP

There are many free online survey programs that allow individuals to create surveys (anonymous or named) to send to a group. The results are organized and shared with the survey maker. Making the survey is very easy, and students often enjoy the "official" appearance of a survey on the screen.

- Interest inventories can take different forms, depending on the age group, the task, and the subject. For book clubs, interest inventories might involve doing a book pass for students to select their book choices from several available selections. For a science experiment, students may select from a variety of materials or hypotheses to demonstrate. At the start of the year, it might through be a survey that students can let you know what subjects, topics, book genres, etc. they are into.
- If you are using an interest inventory as a gauge for student interest around a subject, it is more timely to do the interest inventory after frontloading activities, as students might not initially have the background knowledge to know what they motivated by.
- Ensure that your interest inventory offers a broad range of choice for the students. Whenever possible, especially with written inventories, include space for students to add their own ideas and thoughts.
- Be clear about the purpose of the interest inventory with your students.
- Keep your inventories engaging. Begin with a short task: a 20-minute written survey would undoubtedly squash enthusiasm. If you create a written inventory, make sure there is ample space for writing; tiny boxes and cramped lines are also enthusiasm squashers.

- Use visuals rather than words whenever possible.
- Give consideration to whether the interest inventory should be a whole-class or individual activity. Peers can be powerful influences and can sway friends, especially if they perceive that results of the interest inventory could establish topic groups or reading groups.
- If you are creating a whole-class interest inventory, find a visible space in the classroom to display it. Place a pile of sticky notes beside the inventory and actively encourage students to add their ideas.

CLOSURE

Keep thinking about it! Most interest inventories are not meant to be a one-time check-in, so make time to return to the interest inventory so ideas can be added, subtracted, and modified. Interest inventories can be a powerful tool for directing your curriculum and motivating students. They help students think deeply about what motivates them and can open their minds to new possibilities and ideas. Taking time to home in on the interests of our students is at the crux of student-driven learning.

Treat Learning Like a Continual Treasure Hunt

Encourage students to keep track of their learning, not as a competition or assessment, but to provide a map of learning throughout their year. Making the learning visual and our students aware of their knowledge-gathering helps build their sense of wanting to learn more. We want our students to run home and yell, "Guess what I learned today!" instead of having the often ill-fated dinner conversation, scrambling to recall something to appease their parents' question. Here are some strategies to help make the learning visual:

- The classic K-W-L chart (Ogle, 1986) that marks what a student Knows, Wonders about, and has Learned in a three-column chart can provide a basic outline to show development throughout a unit of study.
- A Friday letter, in which the week is reflected on and shared as a letter to the parents about things that were done and knowledge that was gained.

POSTCARD FROM THE CLASSROOM

Teacher Lisa Fleming has her students share their knowledge in weekly letters and asks parents to respond with their learning through the week.

Very Important: Don't bother doing an interest inventory if you know that your activity or task has constraints that will limit student input. Why poll students on their favorite genres if you know that you have only fairy tales to read?

- A map at the beginning of a geography unit that gives students a chance to add their ideas. As time goes on, have them continue to add or modify in a new color to show the growth of their ideas.
- A class mind map or concept-attainment map at the start of the unit. As the unit progresses, add more ideas using visuals and words. As a class, sort and rearrange the ideas, making connections and modifying the understanding of the concepts. If students have a weekly computer schedule, the first 10 minutes of each class can be given as an opportunity for them to add to the individual mind maps on their unit of study. Let them build their understanding of terms and make their own connections.

Extrinsic and Intrinsic Motivation

Many researchers have had a lot to say about educators who offer rewards as incentives in their classroom. Apparently it doesn't work; yet many teachers can attest to the gleam in students' eyes as they get a sticker on their My Reading chart. So who's right? There are days when I would like to challenge a researcher to spend a week with my students and see if they still think stickers and classroom reward charts aren't the answer to maintaining order (and teacher sanity). So what is motivation?

Motivation is desire and action toward a goal-directed behavior. In a classroom, motivation can be seen as the urge a student has to complete his or her first chapter book, for example.

Intrinsic motivation is when the desire for change comes from within an individual. The motivating factors are internal. An intrinsically motivated student might want to complete that first chapter book because that is something that really interests him or her.

Extrinsic motivation is when the desire for change comes from external factors, such as a prize, bribery, or even punishment. An externally motivated student might want to complete that first chapter book because the teacher has offered prizes to the student who finishes the most books.

A more careful look into the research would indicate that we (researchers and educators) are not so far off in our understanding of what motivates our students. External rewards do work—those stickers can change behaviors and help books get read. But unless our students develop an understanding of how their improved behavior has made their life easier or they were lucky to find the right "hook" book, the benefits of the external motivators are temporary. After a while, stickers by themselves do little to instill a change in attitudes.

As educators, we need to consider how what we do to foster motivation in our classroom. Think about the stickers, the class prizes, the candy draws—what really got the students interested? Ultimately, was it the prize itself, or was it the process of working toward the prize? If we encourage students who care about only the reward, we have created students who will be quickly frustrated at any challenge and will consistently seek the easiest possible way to achieve their goal (the prize). If we encourage students who care more about the process, we have begun to cultivate self-engaged learners.

The relationship between student-driven learning and intrinsic motivation is a cyclical one. In order for student-driven learning to be successful, our students need to be involved in their learning because they are personally interested; this growing interest plants the seeds of intrinsic motivation.

Extrinsic Motivation	To Intrinsic Motivation
• Teacher provides stickers for positive student behavior.	• Student self-identifies one behavior to change and has a weekly conference with teacher (high-need or very young students will need more frequent check-ins).
• Individual reading-reward charts qualify student for a free _____.	• Students keep individual reading logs to record number of books or to share their opinion on a recent read.
• Pizza party as reward for class fundraising.	• Determining a charity to donate to and learning more about it in a meaningful way that connects the students to the cause.
• The quickest finishers get a reward; the slowest finishers get a punishment.	• Understanding and knowing our students enough to create tasks that are open for various learners without a "finished" objective.
• Class that does not show good listening skills stays in for recess.	• Reviewing what listening is and should sound like with the class; also taking a moment to reflect on our own style and if our expectations were reasonable.

On the Straight Road: When Tangible Rewards Work

When learning has a linear progression, extrinsic motivation does work. The carrot on the stick or promise of a prize at the finish line will encourage the student to travel in a linear motion. What tasks involve linear motion? In education, there are a few. These tasks do not require creative thinking or critical questioning, but often involve rote learning. There is little variance expected in the outcome of the task; e.g., memorizing times tables or learning to print on the line are tasks that have one learning path and one learning outcome.

Providing small rewards for these linear tasks will help motivate the students. Provided the task has been carefully constructed so that all students will find some degree of success in the learning progression, a sticker or a prize might make the difference between students who know their times tables and those who do not. We must recognize that providing rewards based on outcome can set up some students for failure. We need to think about ways to ensure that all students in the classroom can achieve the award within a suitable amount of time, and ensure that no one student feels isolated while attempting or accomplishing the task.

ALTERNATIVES TO STICKERS AND SUCKERS

Depending on your educational era, gold stars might be a standard reward for a job well done. Now, there is an entire sticker industry built around education—GOOD JOB, EXCELLENTE, BIEN, and all kinds of positive catch phrases encased in apples, glittery teddy bears, and bumpy lizard stickers. The industry has even bumped it up a notch to include stickers for those students who haven't quite got it yet—ALMOST THERE, GOOD TRY, YOU'RE GETTING IT. I used to agonize about the feedback stickers I gave my students. And then I just stopped using them.

Another popular choice was the sucker. What child (or adult) doesn't leap to receive a candy prize? With the promise of a little sugar, most students will do almost anything—even hand-sharpen a class set of pencils. Obvious drawbacks of a class full sugar-hyped children with cavities in their teeth made me rethink the candies. As well, with rising rates of obesity, dietary restrictions, and cost, food prizes quickly become complicated.

So…what prizes can we, as teachers, dangle at the finish line? Here are a few alternatives, brought to you by the audience you want to hear from—students:

- *Once a week, we are given 15 minutes of free choice, if we get all of our work completed.* (Grade 5)
- *When we have finished our cursive writing book, we receive our pen licence that allows us to write in pen.* (Grade 4)

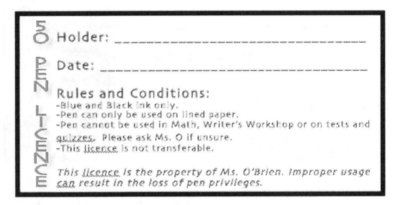

- *My teacher has "bonus bucks" that we can earn when we have a clean desk or don't forget our materials. We can use them to "purchase" choice activities at the end of the month.*
- *We get a homework pass, and it lets us choose one piece of homework to leave incomplete.* (Grade 6)
- *We collect marbles when we show examples of following our class expectations. Once we've gathered enough marbles, we can draw an activity stick (we all choose our favorite class activities at the start of the year) and we get to do that activity.*
- *If we work together to clean up the room quickly, we get more time during our Build It time.* (Grade 1)
- *I can choose my free-choice activity first.* (Kindergarten)

Play as Motivation

One of the purest examples of intrinsic motivation at work can be found in play. Why? Play is fun—and fun is reward enough to continue to play. But in a traditional classroom play is something children do at recess. Recently Ontario has advocated for full-day Kindergarten with a play-based approach to learning. Research has revealed that, contrary to the idea of fun as a distraction, play actually is a powerful motivator for inspiring and engaging our students in their learning.

Mr. V.'s JK/SK class incorporates a play-based approach to learning. Students visit different centres where they explore, experiment, and learn. The Show Table is a spot where students can display their creations. With invented spelling, the students write their own label to accompany their machines.

Promote *Hard Fun* in the Classroom

Seymour Papert, an MIT educator, coined the term "hard fun" (1996). Through researching children's engagement with computers, he realized that learning can be fun because it is hard, it is challenging, and it stretches our capabilities.

When you look at the learning diversity within one classroom, it is tempting to create learning experiences that will allow all students to find success quickly. While these experiences might allow students to gain some satisfaction, this kind of learning can quickly become boring. How can we scaffold learning that is both challenging and within the abilities of our students?

Medium-sized Drive: Selecting Appropriate Home Reading

DESTINATION

Students create and/or select a book for home reading that fits their abilities and interests.

SHIFT

In some classrooms, students are assigned books based on their reading levels and others are allowed to randomly select from a reading bin. Assigning a book can discourage engagement in students' reading, while allowing for random selection might not motivate some students to read more-challenging books.

At the beginning of the reading program, ask students how they would like to select their books for home reading. Odds are, they will want free rein.

UNFOLDING THE ROADMAP

- Create a structure for the books. In younger primary grades or in classrooms where there is a large range of reading levels, bins based on reading levels can help students choose an appropriate book. For students in classes with more-established reading routines where readers are flourishing, bins based on interest or authors might be more appealing to the students.
- Ask students how they would like to set up the bins and make them active participants in the process. This will also give them an opportunity to preview many of the texts.
- Complement the home reading selection with criteria. To begin, it can be about gauging if the book is an appropriate fit, based on reading level or interest. The criteria can be shared in a written format (paper, blog, class website) or with a quick check-in as students grab a new read.
- Create a routine and provide time for children to grab a new book during a set window of time, such as each morning as they arrive, after lunch, or before heading home.
- During book-selection time, ensure an activity is keeping the class working— e.g., quiet reading, writing homework in their agenda, completing a task that can be interfered with—so that you have a chance to touch base with each child. A quick touch-in sounds like this: *Are you still reading X? Was it a good fit? What type of book would you like next?*
- While students are selecting their books, stay aware of their reading level and what might be a good fit as well.
- Empower students to manage their reading by balancing it with other commitments.

POSTCARD FROM THE CLASSROOM

In my Grade 1 class, balancing reading with other activities means that students need to be thinking of their nightly routines and what kind of book might fit in. On evenings a student has a hockey practice, an easier book is a good fit. Students with a lighter schedule may enjoy more of a challenge.

CLOSURE

By allowing our students to select their own texts, we are placing our faith in their judgment. However, we are also meddling in their lives, as we sort the texts into appropriate selections, listen to their responses, help them assess what would be the next step, and guide them toward the next choice. We are empowering them and teaching them to select appropriate challenges.

DETOUR: ADVOCATING FOR CHANGE… ONE CLICK AT A TIME

Twelve-year-old Noah Lahmide began his blog (http://dreamcatcher.bbnow.org/) two years ago. Initially it was part of a community-service project to fund projects for people in need. Through donations to his blog, Noah raised enough money to stop the bank's foreclosure on his grandmother's house. Martha Payne, a nine-year-old British girl, began her blog to comment on the cafeteria lunches at her school (http://neverseconds.blogspot.ca/). Kids all over the world began posting their thoughts as well. With the international attention and more than six million hits, Martha managed to raise money for a charity that provides school lunches to children in need. Martha and Noah are among many youngsters who have become famous for their use of social media to promote positive change.

A powerful element in intrinsic motivation is the understanding that our actions can cause change. Working toward a goal or a purpose is true motivation and something we are seeing more and more in our changing world. The goals of the past—to be rich and have a good job—are not creating satisfied individuals. The Internet is a space where the world shares what they know in an unprecedented way: for free. Why? Because our motivations are shifting and we want to do good.

With digital technologies, kids have discovered a powerful voice. They can join and create global online communities. They can research problems they want to solve, and, using online resources, they can look for solutions. Children are no longer just seen; they are bellowing to be heard, and the online world has provided an audience. Through the sharing of stories, we are making connections. It is these connections that prompt further questions and, ultimately, action.

DIGITAL MOTIVATORS

App/Online Program	Description
Blogs	Blogs create a space where people can express their opinions and then others can add their thoughts to the discussion.
Twitter	Tweeting creates a digital diary. People post what they are doing, thinking, etc. for others to follow and read.
Social Gatherings	Social media sites such as emodo are a way for students to connect with those who have similar interests in a safe and secure space. They can use type, graphics, photos, and videos.
Online Chatting	Free programs, such as skype, allow people to connect globally using text and/or video.

A group of Grade 4 students were engaged in their learning about animals. They were frustrated about animal abuse and took the initiative to create a video about animal rights to share with the school.

Independent Goal-Setting

"Twenty years from now, you will be more disappointed by the things you do than the things you didn't do."
— Mark Twain

Setting goals is an obvious step in creating motivated students. If we set our own goal, we will immediately become completely engaged and work toward achieving that goal. Of course we will all find success at the end of the process; that is, until a great TV show comes on, or we see a piece of chocolate cake, or it is too cold for a run, or we just don't feel like it. As is demonstrated every year by mid-January, resolutions are challenging to keep. If we, as adults, struggle to set manageable goals, we cannot assume that it is an easy task for our students.

Knowing how to set a goal is a skill that must be taught. Goals need to be powerful, meaningful, and realistic. We need to teach our students to set goals to create a future they are excited about, not just one we dream about—not all goals can be around keeping clean desks and neat handwriting.

Types of Goals

There are two types of goals that come into play in our classrooms.

PERFORMANCE GOALS

Performance goals work well for a carrot-and-stick task, one for which the objective is straightforward, is based on memorization, and does not imply creativity or problem-solving. Examples of performance goals:

- memorizing spelling words for a list
- printing neatly
- keeping our desks clean
- getting an A on a test that requires memorization

Performance goals are ideal for reward-based goal programs. These goals have a concrete process, are linear, and require little critical thought or creativity. A small reward, such as a sticker or a stamp, actually makes the task into a game. It heightens the level of enjoyment and challenge.

LEARNING GOALS

Learning goals are just that, a chance to learn. The objective is also straightforward; however, the path to get there is less linear. If the task is to get an A on a French test, it is a performance goal; if the task is to speak French, it is a learning goal. A learning goal can be specific, such as learning a certain science concept, or more wide-ranging, such as playing the piano. For learning goals, a reward system is ineffective. To foster a learning goal, we can have our students share it or we can write it down and later come back to reflect on their growth over time. It is not an immediate response and the process is equally important as the end objective.

BLACK HOLES

Then there are the black holes of motivation, the goals that suck the life out of the learning process:

Being Best: "I want to be the best at math." This goal is completely out of the hands of the student. Who knows what math geniuses are in the classroom? What does it mean to be the best? Is it whoever participates the most? The best at getting all the answers right? The fastest to solve a problem? How do you become the best in math? Do you want to be the best in math in one class? All year? Forever?

First Placers: "I am going to come in first in running." What if the fastest kid in the world comes to your school? How are you going to get fast? What if it is raining when you run your race? What if your shoes are too small? Who are you going to try to beat? When do you want to come in first?

Being Perfect: This concept implies that there is a perfect and ideal way to be. Breaking our students of this mindset is essential. Our students need to know that what they would like to do, they can. At the same time, they need to understand what they want to do. Fostering a sense of independence goes far in creating individuals who are comfortable with their identity and create goals that are in line with their understanding of themselves.

Goal-setting Models

Using a goal-setting program and asking students to track their goal process often rely on performance goals: we want our students to learn how to build on success and students need that to be tangible—they need to see the result. As they become more aware of their learning process and how a growth mindset can reap rewards, they can start to get the big picture of learning goals. We can take our learning goals and break them into manageable chunks: e.g., the learning goal is to read, so the performance goal to match that would be for students to ensure they are reading 15 minutes each night. Chunking learning goals does not always translate coherently, but it does help our students understand that they can grow their minds and work toward achieving an end result.

Acronyms are handy ways for students to remember what qualifies as a realistic and achievable performance goal. The following acronyms can be used as a starting point for creating one personalized for your class.

1. Goals can be SMART:
   Specific
   Measurable
   Achievable
   Realistic
   Timely
   Adapted from Meyer (2006)

2. The ABC of Goals:
   Attainable
   Believable
   Concrete

POSTCARD FROM THE CLASSROOM

Reflecting Back, looking forward

Name: _____|___   Date: _____

Highlights of the year so far...

_____

Think back to your hope and goals from Term 1, which ones have already been realized?

_____

Choose 2 goals for Term 2. Fill out the Goal-Setting chart.

Goal	My action plan to reach my goal	How will I know I have reached my goal?

This is a sample of a Grade 5 goal-setting sheet. It is filled out by the student and used for a student-led conference.

Big Journey: Goal-setting in the Classroom

DESTINATION

To give our students the tools to set realistic, personal goals that will help focus their motivation and support their learning journey.

SHIFT

We know the curriculum and the abilities of our student, so wouldn't it be easiest if we set the goals? This attitude does little to inspire individual students. Students need to be empowered with the ability to decide what is an important goal for them. While we can ask our students to justify their ideas, we can never underestimate their need for change.

SPARK

Ask students: *What does it mean to make a goal? Who do you want to be right now? What adjectives would you want someone to use to describe you?*

UNFOLDING THE ROADMAP

- Brainstorm ideas for a teacher's goals. What kinds of goals should a teacher want? Record students' responses.
- Share some Black Holes (see page 56) with the students: e.g., I want to be the best teacher; I was to be a perfect teacher. Discuss why these kinds of goals might be difficult to achieve.
- Create a checklist with the class about what an achievable goal might need. You may want to use the SMART outline or the ABC of Goals to help (see page 57).
- Ask students to create their own goals. You might want to initially do this as a whole-class activity. It can help students to see what other students are aspiring to.
- Start with one goal per student. Anything more is difficult to track and achieve.
- Have students check goals against the checklist with a partner.
- Create a plan for achieving the goal. Record this plan, paying special attention to the timeline. Include an image of the plan.
- Give students a cue card, sticky note, sentence strip, or some other means of documenting their goal. Place the goal in a prominent spot in the classroom or on individual desks.
- Decide on a way of monitoring the goal; e.g., through a weekly check-in, peer motivation buddies, class meetings…whatever works best for your class.

CLOSURE

Check-ins are essential for ensuring that the goals do not blend into the wall display and become forgotten. Make sure your students keep their goals simple and straightforward. At the start of the process, student success makes future goal-setting easier. Goal-setting needs to be ongoing throughout the year and developed into a meaningful part of your practice; otherwise, students will quickly see that their goals are not valued and reinforced.

In my classroom, the students come up with one manageable performance goal. We brainstorm goals that can be achieved a few times a day, such as writing neatly, changing quickly for physical education, using the word wall to spell familiar words. The students write the goals and place them on their desks. As the day passes, if they decide they have achieved a goal, they share their accomplishment with any teacher or adult in the room and can grab a sticker and place it on the goal. Making the students responsible for monitoring their own goals manages 30 individual goals as well as building intrinsic motivation. It is also wonderful to hear six-year-olds come up to you throughout the day and say, "I achieved my goal."

Resurfacing: Emotional Buoyancy and Risk-taking

> "Be who you are and say what you feel, because those who mind don't matter and those who matter don't mind."
> — Dr. Seuss

Creating a classroom infused with student-driven learning demands that students be willing to take risks daily, hourly, and sometimes every minute. A motivated and engaged student will welcome the opportunity to take a risk; however, to want to take a risk, students must feel motivated and engaged. This powerful circle of influences is a relationship that we need to be ever mindful of. There are many factors that can influence our students' emotional buoyancy:

CLEAR SKIES AHEAD
- Having the know-how to do what you want to do
- Seeing the value in the task
- Being able to focus on the task
- Knowing the plan for moving forward to complete the task
- Understanding how to prioritize what needs to be done
- Persistence

BOULDERS
- Feeling anxious
- Feeling frustrated
- Concern about disappointing teachers/peers/parents
- Believing that, no matter what the outcome (positive or negative), you have little control

So should all learning tasks guarantee immediate success for our students? In the realm of student-driven learning, should we encourage our students to always choose easily accessible learning goals? The obvious answer is no. But if we are going to ask that our students undertake academic challenges, we need to cultivate a learning environment that promotes risk-taking and emotional buoyancy.

Emotional buoyancy refers to our ability to deal with difficult setbacks in our lives. It is incredibly easy to feel motivated when everything is going our way, but how do we respond when things are not going our way? It is at these crossroads that you can see anxiety and frustration emerge in your students. Some students independently work past these boulders and find their route forward. But other students quickly become disengaged and abandon the task or goal altogether. How can we develop emotional buoyancy in our students?

Big Journey: Bouncing Back

DESTINATION

To give students the emotional toolkit to help them persist when their goals are not easily met.

SHIFT

If you control the learning tasks, you can orchestrate it so that your students have a greater chance of immediate success. You can also quickly intervene and redirect wayward students toward your predetermined outcome. But what happens when students do not reach the outcome easily? What happens when you inadvertently create a learning task that is too challenging? Regardless of the teaching approach used in the classroom, students need to develop resilience and persistence. In a student-driven learning environment, emotional buoyancy is essential to student success.

SPARK

At school, who are our Success Assassins? Success Assassins are those things or people—tangible or not—that influence our ability to reach our goals. (I have to invent names for them; the students love when we give their nemeses names.) Here is a list of some suspected Success Assassins:

- Misunderstando—"I don't get it."
- Boringado—"I find this task boring."
- Explosiviva—"There is too much noise; I can't focus."
- Prezzure—"I am being pressured by outside forces, like my parents, teachers, friends, etc. to do well or not do well."
- Blankster—"I just can't think of a new idea."
- Strezzi—"Something is making me feel anxious and I can't pay attention."

UNFOLDING THE ROADMAP

- Take a look at Success Assassins. Discuss why these things bring us down and make learning difficult.
- Divide up the list of Assassins and have students come up with one bad guy to fight. Some students might want to draw the assassin and give a visual to the bad guy.
- Bring students back together and have them share their ideas on how they can fight the Assassins. Record their ideas and post them in the classroom. Including visual images—e.g., a bouncing ball, a "knock-out" comic font, a boxing glove—on a poster will help make the ideas more memorable.

With younger children, you might want to use a different term, such as Success Squashers. But trust me, older children will really love to imagine Success Assassins as super-villains.

- When a student gets taken down by one of the Assassins—and it will happen—refer to the ideas of how to overcome the challenges. With each scenario, you will likely be able to add to the class ideas.
- Continue to model the language of Success Assassination in the classroom with safe examples, such as your own anecdotes or whole-class examples.
- As the process develops, shift the focus from the assassins to the solutions. Make the solutions the big deal, as these are the things we can do to bounce back. If you are using the bad guy/good guy theme, the solutions can be heroes.
- Celebrate students who overcome challenges and, if they are comfortable, allow them to share their experiences.
- Track the heroes, making the learning visible. If anyone in the classroom overcomes an Assassin, share it aloud, putting a star next to the visual or adding a box to the graph you are creating to track positive change.

CLOSURE

While this idea is simple for students, it provides kid-friendly vocabulary to describe their feelings of frustration and failure. It can help deflect the attention away from personalizing these negative feelings and instead allow these feelings to be directed toward the "Assassins." This process needs to be modelled, discussed, and reflected upon often.

Assertive Inquiry

Teacher Erica Sprules works to build resilience in her Grade 2 students by teaching them *assertive inquiry*. She has coined the term to refer to an active, engaged process to inquiry. It is a mode of communication that involves the explicit expression of one's ideas and the sincere exploration of another's. It is a key component of the Integrative Thinking decision-making model devised by the Rotman School of Management.

There are two parts to assertive inquiry: the explicit expression of one's ideas (sharing ideas) and the exploration of another's ideas (asking questions). Erica models assertive inquiry with her students and has prompts written on cue cards so they can refer to them during their discussion. Here are some sample prompts for asking questions:

- *Can you explain…?*
- *What do you think…*
- *Why…?*

Here are some sample prompts for sharing ideas:

- *I think…*
- *The reason I think that is…*
- *My idea is…*

Get Help in Building Student Resiliency

"Yes, you've been pampered, cosseted, doted upon, helmeted, bubble-wrapped. But do not get the idea you're anything special. Because you're not."
—From David McCullough's 2012 commencement speech

David McCullough's 2012 commencement speech at Wellesley High School in Boston made international news. Some were horrified that the English teacher would dare to leave the graduating students with the message that they were not special and unique; others acknowledged he possibly was right. It is said that our students are growing up in the age of entitlement. What they want, they get, and often they have a team of adults supporting their desires. With helicopter parenting whirring its way into our classrooms, teachers are also being expected to hover over our students, offering up a stream of reassurance and encouragement. It is a predictable equation: encouragement and reassurance beget the need for more encouragement and reassurance.

As teachers, we know that the students who wake up every morning to parents sorting their backpacks and laying out their clothes are going to be the same students who struggle to find pencils, cannot locate their homework, and ask how to complete a task before even beginning. A big part of building resilience in our students begins at home. But how can we build confidence and resilience in our students' lives outside of school? Here are a few teacher tips for building resilience in your parent community:

- Begin early, on the first day, with a warm smile, and shut your door once the school bell rings. Allow students to be independent of their parents in the classroom.
- Stand at your door, not behind your desk. While no one wants to appear to be the gatekeeper, standing at the door allows you to gently stop parents from entering your class without speaking with you first. Make sure you are clear that your role at the door is to greet students, not overhear parents' concerns.
- Set up a policy for how you will handle forgotten work and other items. I tell parents that there is almost nothing so important it can't be brought in the next day—with the exception of a lunch! If a child has forgotten something, ensure the parents do not drop it off in the classroom, but instead have them leave it at the office where the student can pick it up.
- Inform parents early and let the kids speak for themselves. Parents get worried when they don't know what is going on. Put the responsibility on the students to bring notes/permission forms home. If a parent e-mails or calls about an event, ask the parent to speak to the child first and to call back if there is need for further clarification.
- Unfinished work? Mishap at school? Let your students talk with their parents first. In Kindergarten, my son wrote a note home about a missing book. He had ownership of the problem and spent his playtime looking for that book.
- When providing positive or negative feedback to a parent, ensure that the student is an active part of the conversation.
- As students grow older, identify getting-ready-for-school tasks that can be easily done by the kids. Share these with the parents and kids.

POSTCARD FROM THE CLASSROOM

When it comes time for a field trip, I ensure my students play an active part of preparing for that day. We sit down together and look over the weather and itinerary. The students brainstorm a list of the clothing they will need, along with any other items. If the list has key items, they write them down. I also ask them to pack for themselves. Although I cannot guarantee that this is happening, it gives the students a feeling of empowerment when I communicate to them that they are capable. If a parent asks what might be needed, I refer them to the child as the person who is responsible. Items forgotten by children who packed for themselves present a valuable life lesson and will go far to ensure they are better planned for the next trip.

As teachers, we do have a role in inspiring and supporting our students. But we have an equally important role in ensuring that they learn how to give and respond to criticism. Creating a caring classroom where students learn to offer both encouragement and critical commentary helps prepare resilient students.

The Language of Gratitude

Being motivated, engaged, and resilient is not a constant state. We all have days when we feel completely shattered and think that life hasn't turned out how we expected. Building emotional buoyancy helps us know that challenging times last only so long. But even this knowledge isn't always enough. As educators, we need a classroom that embodies positive thought. While it might be a simple idea, there is much power in using the language of gratitude to help create a positive classroom environment.

What does gratitude look like in our classrooms? Beginning in reverse, gratitude is not empty praise or instant thanks. It is being thankful and being able to return thanks. Unlike praise, it is long-lasting and meaningful. When we are grateful to somebody or for something, we tend to hold these experiences in our memory. It is through our connection to these memories that we will often react in a positive way toward someone or something. Gratitude is the bridge that connects us to each other.

In our classrooms, gratitude is…

- Speaking in a positive tone
- Thanking people and situations
- Having thoughts that are positive and full of wonder
- Feeling energetic and involved
- Being motivated to help others
- Believing that we are lucky to be part of this class

To build gratitude in a classroom, the teacher needs to model and practice giving and receiving thanks—not just with students, but with colleagues as well. It is not lavishing unnecessary praise on our students, but is instead watching carefully for small acts of kindness and recognizing those acts. It does not have to be a bulletin board of thanks or a thank-you gift certificate; just a simple verbal expression of thanks is enough. In return, our students not only should be the receivers of thanks, but also need to be encouraged and taught how to express their thanks.

Here are some simple ways to encourage the language of thanks in your classroom:

1. At the start of the year, begin by thanking your students for being part of the classroom.
2. Once school has begun, have small meetings with groups of students and ask them what they are happy about in the classroom. In turn, reflect on positive things you are seeing.
3. Call/write parents and recall one positive anecdote about each child. Don't make this conversation about anything else.
4. When working together, give students sentence prompts to help them express their gratitude; for example,

   - *I really enjoyed working with you because…*

- *It was fun when we _____ed together.*
- *I thought you worked well at…*
- *I would like to work with you again because…*
- *You are really great at…*

5. At the end of group work, ask every group to think of one high-five for their group. Don't follow this up with one critique; save that for another conversation.
6. Have a daily quote for the students that focuses on gratitude.
7. Share stories from the news about individuals or groups who are helping others.
8. Encourage staff to visit your room and give positive feedback (when deserved) to the students. In turn, visit your colleagues' classrooms with the same intent.
9. Send a small treat to colleagues and have students deliver the treat!
10 Write thank-you cards as a class to volunteers who come in to help.
11. As part of the reflection process, ask students what they are thankful for.

Small Hop: The Power of the Sunshine Call

DESTINATION

To make a positive connection with parents/guardians about their child.

SHIFT

Between e-mails, texts, mail, phones, and personal contact, there are many ways to connect to our parent community. It is very common for a teacher to contact home if there is a concern or an incident. A Sunshine Call is contact with parents to share a positive moment about their child. The Sunshine Call is a moment to celebrate the child, with no other intent.

SPARK

Can you find one positive anecdote to tell about every student in your class? Can you make a connection to each student, something special that each has said or done in the school?

UNFOLDING THE ROADMAP

- The Sunshine Call is a powerful tool, because it instantly says

    I care about your child.
    I celebrate your child.
    We (child, teacher, and parent) are each equal forces and we share information.
    I am working with your child to create more Sunshine moments.

- Try to make your Sunshine Calls within the first few months of school. The early good news can establish a trusting and positive relationship between you, the child, and the family.
- Making 32 phone calls is a daunting task. Do not try to do all the calls at once. Choose five or six calls to make at a time.
- If parents/guardian are not at home to receive a phone call, follow up with an e-mail. The e-mail can be of similar format to e-mails you send to other parents/guardians but it should include a personalized positive moment. It cannot

include anything other than the item being celebrated, and definitely nothing critical or negative.

- If possible, let the students know you will be calling. Students might need to translate the call or might be able to let you know when their parents/guardians will be in.
- Make the call quick and to the point, sharing a positive moment from the day.

CLOSURE

There is no way to get around the time issue. Making personal phone calls/e-mails takes time. But the reward is undeniable, as students know that you understand them and parents/guardians feel that you have a vested interest in their child's learning.

Don't despair when the thanks your students begin with is superficial; to build an environment of gratitude takes time. Even the sarcastic "thanks" will eventually change with modelling and practice. Take it easy—enjoy your job, your students, and your school. On those days when the photocopier is broken and no one refilled the coffee in the staff room, make sure you have a stash of chocolate ready to remind you that these bad moments come and go quickly. Pull out your favorite read-aloud or put on a great song and just take it easy. Reports, reading assessments, professional development, hounding parents, grumpy colleagues, broken photocopiers…they can all wait. Take a deep breath, shut the classroom door, crank up the music, and be grateful.

5

Getting Off the Linear Path

I was walking through a school with my son and we came across a bulletin board with art pictures that all replicated each other. Each drawing was a child's attempt to copy the same picture, from the curves to the lines and the detail, but in a different color. The teacher's demonstration model was also posted. Dean, who was five at the time, looked at the bulletin board and turned to explain it to me. "Mommy, it is a competition. The teacher draws a picture and everyone has to do the same one to see who is the best. But the teacher is always the best."

— A parent

"Do not go where the path may lead; go instead where there is no path and leave a trail."
— Ralph Waldo Emerson

Teaching our students to learn means showing them how to find their own way to solve problems, how to meet set criteria by being creative. Learning becomes an active process. Their product will not all be the same, there will be no teacher model to copy, and we will learn with them as they find ways to think that we have not yet encountered.

We could sit our students down, show them the curriculum, explain to them the objectives, and start on a linear path. This will produce a set outcome and we can assess our students on how well they copied our lines and detail, how well they replicated us. As an alternative, we can provide them the objective and allow them to determine how to meet it, what line, color, or detail to use and include. They can incorporate new ideas and demonstrate how they met the criteria on their own path. It is through this kind of exploration that we empower our students.

This chart gives examples of the difference between teaching as leading students down a linear path and learning as students finding their own way:

Expectation	Linear Path	Carving Their Own Path
Editing for capitals, periods, punctuation in sentence writing	Students are given a worksheet with prepared sentences to edit.	Students are told to write a sentence containing two errors. All sentences are placed in a bin and students draw sentences for which they must find the errors. The original writer and the editor meet to discuss the sentence and share it when it has met their criteria.

Expectation	Linear Path	Carving Their Own Path
Use of various lines in art (linking to fairytale unit; using dragons)	Students are shown how to draw various lines. The teacher models how to use the lines to draw a dragon; students are given time to replicate the posted drawing of a dragon using the lines.	Students are shown how to draw various lines. They create a list of what a dragon has (scales, eyes, wings, etc.). They are challenged to create a fantastic monster (preferably not a dragon) using the different lines.
Understanding the feudal system during the medieval era	Students are told how the feudal system worked and given a task to retell what they were just told.	Students select a role in feudal society. They research what their position would be like. Students determine if they would like to be in that position; they justify their reasoning.
Mental math facts for addition to 10	Students are given a series of worksheets or dice and asked to practice their math facts.	Students are presented with the objective and a variety of games and tasks (devised by teacher and students) and they decide how they would like to practice.

DETOUR: ALGORITHMIC VS HEURISTIC WORK

The US consulting firm McKinsey & Co. estimates that today 30% of job growth is from algorithmic work while the other 70% comes from heuristic work. (McKinsey Quarterly 4, 2005, as quoted in Pink, 2009: 25–26)

By following the linear path, we are completing algorithmic tasks. Algorithmic work is manual or procedural task-driven work. This kind of task has people wrapping chocolates as they come out the of the machine or children following the prescribed steps to make a Lego car. People doing algorithmic work are replicating what has and can be done by others. These tasks are routine, involved, and repetitive; they require less individual thought.

When we challenge our students to create their own path, they are completing heuristic tasks. This kind of task includes designing new logos for a product and thinking of ways to solve problems. People doing heuristic work are required to think creatively, or outside of the box, to build on ideas. These are the tasks assigned to our white-collar workers in the hopes of producing unique results to push companies forward. In our students, heuristic tasking creates a sense of empowerment, motivation, drive, and ultimately satisfaction.

For our students to be successful, they need to hone their creative skills and develop heuristic work skills. Using backward design as our model, how do we ensure our students meet this goal? How do we prepare them for their future? What pushes our students off the traditional path and helps them create their own routes?

Autonomy: A Detour Off the Linear Path

As teachers, when we enter our classrooms and face our students, we have autonomy. We are guided by curriculum and supported by management, but how we teach is largely up to us. This is one of the most important factors in job satisfaction, not just in the classroom, but also in the business world. Major companies around the world have noted that giving employees autonomy over their roles means they solve more problems and create more interesting products than they would under the paycheque- and monitoring-management systems of the past. Google, 3M, and Atlassian have given employees 20% of their time to create, and each company has cited that their most innovative products and ideas come from this creative time. Yet how much autonomy are we giving our students? When we trust our students and provide them the space to think, we are giving them autonomy.

Imagine if someone told Pablo Picasso, Dr. Seuss, or any one of us that we needed to follow the lines and complete the task just like everyone else. Autonomy is essential for the sense of freedom we require. It is essential for creating new ideas and for developing creativity. With student-driven learning, we provide our students with the opportunity to respond to problems in their own way and to think. We are telling our students that we value their ideas and are giving them space to experiment, play, and try out their theories.

POSTCARD FROM THE CLASSROOM

In art, students from Kindergarten to Grade 5 read Peter Reynold's *The Dot*. Afterward, they were given all kinds of materials and asked to make their own mark. The only criterion was that the work had to be different from anyone else's. These were hung for all to see near the art room.

For more about autonomy, read *Drive* by Daniel Pink.

According to a cluster of recent studies in behavioral science, students who have more autonomy also have

- higher self-esteem
- better interpersonal relationships
- greater conceptual understanding
- getter grades
- enhanced persistence at school and in activities
- higher productivity
- less burnout
- greater levels of psychological well-being

Small Hop: Brainstorming Starting Routines

DESTINATION

To empower students to create routines that help the school year flow.

SHIFT

Rather than outlining a rotational schedule for feeding the class pet, washroom breaks, or use of highly coveted device, allow students the opportunity to create the system. They are thinking critically about a washroom pass or feeding a class pet because we empowered them to do so.

SPARK

Present the problem: *Who gets to go to the washroom, when, where? Who gets to feed the pet? There are four computers; how do we make sure everyone gets a chance during free time? How do we make it fair for everyone?* Give students time to think about solutions.

UNFOLDING THE ROADMAP

- Brainstorm ways to solve the problem as a whole. Record and listen to the discussion. Students will probably create a rotational system, based on names on a list.
- As students share their ideas, they will start to evaluate what they think will work (many may like one idea) or critique ideas they have experienced before or doubt. During this dialogue, begin to sort the recorded ideas.
- Narrow down ideas to find the first idea to try. Decide which ones can be determined by a blind vote (heads in lap) or that flow from the discussion.

CLOSURE

By empowering our students to create their own system, we are also opening them up to critical thought. As the year progresses, the system might work well, need to be adapted, or need a complete overhaul. This presents more opportunities for learning. Since students created the system, they are more aware of it, assessing what elements are working and what might need fine-tuning. They can reflect on the system, modify it, and learn from their own decisions.

The reading couch was one of the most coveted places in our classroom. Almost a decade's worth of kid grime covered the couch, but it didn't matter—everyone wanted to sit on the couch. I had created a complicated seating system that used rotational weeks and involved moving clothes pegs. It was a disaster. I decided to turn the problem over to my students. I shared the current dilemma and sent them in small groups to brainstorm possible solutions. They came back with ideas ranging from buying more couches to letting everyone sit on the couch. Despite some of the wild ideas, the students narrowed it down to a few plausible suggestions. The class voted on three possibilities and a small crew of kids came forward to organize a new seating chart that worked on a weekly rotation of three students at a time. It was simple and it worked. The clothes pegs are now being used to hold up that brilliant seating chart.

How to Provide Autonomy in the Classroom

Understanding autonomy is important, but translating that concept into a small room with limited resources and many bodies is challenging. How can we foster autonomy in our classrooms?

PROVIDE CHOICE

When we present students with forks in the road, we allow them to choose their own path. If our path is always linear, at some point our students' passion is going to fizzle out. If the requirement is to write a story, we can provide choice in topic, in means of communicating (written, typed, spoken), and in method of sharing (traditional story, comic, stop-motion animation). Creating and sharing a story is an important skill for every child and adult. Regardless of how a story is created, the process of brainstorming ideas, understanding the elements, creating, and sharing will remain consistent. But by providing choice in creation technique, we give our students a chance at a path they are more eager to take.

When asked *What choices would you like in your classroom?* this is how our students responded:

- *What we play*
- *The type of tests we have, and how often*
- *How we learn our math*
- *The type of work*
- *What we do for our projects*
- *How we want to research*
- *Where we sit*
- *I am ok with teacher choices, as long as I have a voice*
- *We would like one period or class where we can do anything we want, like get caught up on homework*

PROVIDE STRUCTURE

Autonomy is not synonymous with chaos. Ensure that students can understand and follow routines within the classroom. Be considerate about noise level and activity level; many students feel safest in quiet, calm spaces. Decide which activities can be free-rein and which need to be presented in a more structured manner. And while doing all of this, leave a little wiggle room for the exuberant moments.

RELEASE THE TASK

Pure autonomy requires us to release all expectations and to let the students lead the way. This philosophy is supported in many educational systems. For example, in Emilio Reggio students fully take the lead and the teacher's role is to observe, record, and then help foster and direct learning for students. The curriculum is naturally created from the students' interest and developmental needs.

Although this philosophy might seem improbable in education systems that have set criteria to meet, we can take small steps toward releasing the task by piquing the students' interest and putting them back in the driver's seat.

TAKE TIME

All growth needs time. We do not need more time; rather, we need to reevaluate how we are using our time. We have the best part of each day with each student. Replacing tasks that require simple linear movement and skill development with tasks that allow for more autonomy will not only provide our students with time to develop divergent thinking, but will also allow them to master their skill development in ways that support their interests.

MAKE SPACE

Fostering a sense of individual autonomy in a space that is shared by many little and big people can present challenges. Using space wisely is important. Students will need access to independent space where they can find a quiet place to think, even if it is behind or in a cardboard box. They will need spaces to group together and collaborate in both small and larger groups so that they can develop their ideas with others. They will also need space to explore and experiment where they can lay out their plans or test their ideas.

USE TOOLS

Students will need access to all the tools we can provide for them. Understanding where the tools are and how to maintain them is important (from locating pencil baskets and sharpeners to the ability to unlock the iPad storage unit and recharge devices). Students also need to be taught explicitly how to use the tools. While there is always a place for learning through exploration, be mindful of potential frustration when students cannot use the learning tools to their advantage.

TAKE THE LEAP

If we are willing to take the step off the algorithmic ledge and leap onto the heuristic platform, we will find not only that we cover our basic skill development in more interesting and meaningful ways, but also that we create student-driven learners who are empowered, creative, motivated, resilient, and ready to move our future forward.

This picture shows what happened when students decided to claim the bulletin board. They wanted to share in their own way what they were learning about rocks and minerals. They took over the board near the beginning of the unit and added to it, individually or in partners, at their leisure. They shared their knowledge as a picture or a large diagram, adding ideas they learned or questions they had on the little note pads. I viewed the board to check on their understanding and we would use it to begin a new lesson to refresh our concept of what we already knew. The biggest rule about the bulletin board: I was not allowed to touch it. Although it was not as visually appealing as something created by one person, it became a great source of information, with students eagerly running to the hall to check something on it or to add something they just learned.

Medium-sized Drive: Creating a Moment of Autonomy

DESTINATION

To provide our students with the opportunity to explore and learn from their exploration.

SHIFT

Rather than guiding our students through set curriculum objectives, we are using their exploration and wondering to determine what they know and what might be the next steps in their learning. For instance, rather than listing the names, attributes, and properties of something they are learning about, we provide students with the opportunity to take the lead in their learning and create an opportunity to explore.

SPARK

Explain to the students that they have a set amount of time to explore and create using manipulatives appropriate to the topic at hand. They will have access to as many tools as you can provide to explore: pencils, paper, manipulatives, digital apps, computer access—whatever might be appropriate.

UNFOLDING THE ROADMAP

- Ensure that students understand that they can move fluidly from one tool to another. They can work independently or collaboratively, and this might also change as they shift tools and follow their thinking.

- Ensure that students understand that sharing their ideas and observations will also be part of the process, either as a whole group upon completion or as individuals and small groups while circulating.
- Circulate while the students are exploring. Meddle and push their thinking if they are circling one idea or hesitant to take the next step by asking open-ended questions; i.e., "What could you do with this?" Know also when to step back and let them continue on their own when they are independently processing ideas or building on their own thoughts.
- Use a clipboard and checklist to track the ideas the students are covering independently. For instance, learning about 3D shapes, one group might be exploring how the 3D shapes stack or combine while building; an individual could be working with an electronic tool that shows the sides and faces of the shape.
- Know where the gaps might be so they can be filled in later, either with more explanation from you or by pushing an idea that is close a bit closer.
- Bring the group together and share the discoveries. While students share what they explored or learned, collect this information on a class chart or the interactive whiteboard. As the concept is explored further, refer to this chart and adapt or change the information. Build on this knowledge.
- Post results of the exploration as scientific discoveries, with challenges to the class: *Can you also prove this? Do you agree? Do you disagree? What other ways can we show this? How can this be useful if it is true?*

CLOSURE

For more on formative assessment, see The Learning Map (page 104).

You can use this type of exploration as a form of formative assessment or assessment for learning, diving into your students' current understandings of a topic and making an inventory of where to go next. You can use this information to determine what needs to be taught whole-class, gone over with larger groups, covered in small groups, or reviewed individually. Keep the materials close at hand for any students who want to revisit the topic and explore their ideas.

Collaborating: Circular Learning

POSTCARD FROM THE CLASSROOM

While lying on a beach in Florida, Davey said: "Mommy, I miss inquiry." (This was recounted by Davey's mom.) Inquiry in our class is the time when we come together to explore a topic.

Collaboration builds on autonomy. If autonomy means giving our students ownership of their learning, then collaboration means giving our students the resources to build their learning. By collaborating, our students

- Enrich their understanding. By sharing their ideas out loud, they are teaching others what they know or understand. They are moving beyond basic intake of information and reaching that 90% of understanding on Eldon Ekwall's chart (see page 15), reinforcing their learning by using their information to teach others.
- Connect to prior knowledge. Listening critically pushes our students to make branches or connections with what they hear and what they already

know. It builds on their foundation of knowledge and helps them appreciate a new perspective or idea.

- Reevaluate what they know. Revisiting what we believe is an essential part of collaboration. If we do not reevaluate what we know, we will never learn anything new. Our students need to use the information gained in collaboration to alter their current understanding. They can choose to accept it, reject it, or accept parts of it. Regardless of what they decide to do with the new information, the process of deciding how this new knowledge affects their current knowledge forces them to reevaluate their current understanding. It pushes their perspective.

- Listen critically. Collaboration means that our students are listening to others. They are digesting information from their peers with the same interest as (or more interest than) what they show information from their teachers. They look to their peers and teachers as equals in learning, and they are evaluating how this new knowledge influences their current understanding.

Big Journey: How to Listen Critically

DESTINATION

To push our students to listen critically.

SHIFT

We need to listen critically to our students. Rather than assuming that they are blank vessels to be filled, we know that their prior knowledge is important, as it is the base of any further understanding.

SPARK

Post a strong opinion that will elicit a passionate response in your students: e.g., *all students should wear uniforms; computer games create mindless zombies.*

UNFOLDING THE ROADMAP

- Allow a moment for the comment to sink in.
- Draw a line on the floor. At one end post *Strongly Agree*; at the other end, post *Strongly Disagree.*
- Before beginning, distinguish with students the difference between fact and opinion; i.e., they are stating their opinion, and hopefully supporting it with facts.
- Ask students to place themselves on the line. What do they believe?
- Form clumps with students that are close to each other.
- Before encouraging discussion, take the time to reflect on how to have a productive discussion, so that students understand how to support their opinions and listen to others with an open mind.
- Ask students to justify their opinions on the comment. They need to create a few reasons why they put themselves in that spot.
- Have groups share their ideas.
- When everyone has finished, let the class take a moment to think about what was said.
- Give students the opportunity to move to a different location based on new understandings.
- Give them a chance to share why they chose to move, what influenced them, or why they chose to stay where they were.

In the end, we hope our students begin to listen with a more critical ear. To model this and support our student-driven classroom, we also must value each individual idea. In our busy, rushed world it is sometimes easier to keep moving and smile blankly, nod, or lose focus when students are sharing their ideas. When we join them in making the effort to respect each other's ideas and opinions, we foster a more collaborative classroom.

Arrange Desks for Collaboration

In a classroom full of group activities or independent activities, students can use their peers as resources for questions or support. As you shift from a structure in which teachers are the bearers of knowledge to an atmosphere where students learn with and from each other, you need to set up the classroom so that students can communicate with everyone while making eye contact. Desks can be grouped in a variety of arrangements:

- Small groups or clusters. Cluster formation is ideal when working on collaborative tasks in small groupings.
- The U formation. In the U or V formation, students can make eye contact with each other. This arrangement is useful when holding class debates or discussions. The students can access the large centre area for bigger floor projects or a place to come together and talk.
- The reversed U or V formation. Place the desks in the U formation, but with the backs facing the inside of the U. When the class needs to collaborate, they can face each other to talk and discuss. When it comes time for an independent task, students spin their chairs around and face outward, avoiding the distraction of peers.
- A circle. Removing the gap from the U or V formation shifts the classroom's space from one with a set front to a space in which the main focus is collaboration. That said, there needs to be enough space for movement around and through desks so that no one can get trapped in the middle or locked into the neighbors on either side. Just as with the U and V formation, desks can be positioned with fronts in or out.
- Office spaces. Creating a space where students can go to separate their ideas from the classroom of collaboration is valuable. A small office space or quiet area provides this outlet. As well, a quiet space can be accessed when a small group is working together on a difficult problem. The potential of a cardboard box is endless. It can be anything a child can imagine and, when cut open, it can also be transformed into a personal office space. Other options for creating office spaces: voting partitions after a recent election; file folders opened and propped up.
- Collaboration table or space. Depending on the shape of the classroom, there might not be enough flexibility to have everyone in collaborative spaces. A table or floor space opened up somewhere in the room for collaborative work can quickly become a high-traffic area for group brainstorming or laying out collaborative tasks.

Websites like http://classroom. 4teachers.Org/ are great and simple resources to encourage students to design the classroom space.

When asked *How do you like the furniture in the classroom to be arranged?* this is how our students responded:

- *Couches, areas to relax.*
- *The tables should be different colors.*
- *Couches because they are comfortable*
- *Bean bag chairs*
- *There has to be a couch for relaxation*
- *Make it bright, it makes the room more interesting, positive*
- *More variety of books*
- *Everything organized*
- *Mix up the chairs often enough, so we sit with different people*

When presenting a seating arrangement, you can have either predetermined or open seating. Seats with predetermined owners ensure that students know exactly where they sit; this arrangement also acts as a management system, as we can move students so that they work with others or to separate peers from each other. Seats left unassigned allow students to access different spots and partners as the tasks shift, or just keep each day fresh.

At the start of the year it is difficult to know our students, how much they have grown over the summer, and how they will engage in our classroom; it is hard to assess them for a predetermined seating position. Consider starting with open seating, giving them the opportunity to mingle with everyone in the classroom, and giving yourself the chance to assess their behaviors. Some teachers switch up their seating arrangements every day for the first week. Once a few weeks have passed, student engagement in a self-evaluation about where they select to sit and about learning styles will further explore their needs. Student criteria for seating could include which peers assist learning (they can support me or I can review concepts with them) and which location in the room accommodates physical needs. Students need to be able to focus on their academics and make strong social decisions. Deciding where they sit and altering their seating using criteria and reflection helps students think independently.

Mastery from Engagement

The concept of mastery from engagement seems to claim a huge amount. Yet it is true that, when we are fully engaged in an activity, we strive to master it. Think of the child on the skateboard determined to master a trick, even with a broken arm and recovering from a broken ankle. Think of the hook of a good book for a struggling reader. If we are engaged, we want to master the skills needed to perfect what we are interested in. Engagement is key.

The foundation of mastery is the understanding that it is possible. We need to instill in our students the belief that they can do anything. Pushing them in the direction they are driving will require that they can operate the car. Knowing how to steer, shift, read, write, and compute are all skills they can foster to drive more effectively on their path, to move forward. Once they are engaged in moving, they will become passionate about mastering the required skills, without feeling the weight of the word "requirement." If they would like to achieve Z, they can. And while working toward Z, they will also pick up X and Y to make Z possible. It is engagement that ignites mastery.

Medium-sized Drive: Engaging Students in Curricular Objectives

DESTINATION

To share, explore, and meet curriculum objectives with the students.

SHIFT

Rather than using the curriculum as the starting point and letting it guide our teaching, we can use our students' engagement as the starting point and create a checklist of objectives to ensure we meet curricular demands.

SPARK

Select one curriculum objective that requires critical thought; e.g., *Understand how ancient civilizations used their environment.* Present the objective to students and have them create a project or task to demonstrate their learning on this topic.

UNFOLDING THE ROADMAP

- List curricular expectations that involve skill- or knowledge-based learning; e.g., using proper punctuation, recall of basic facts, listing the elements of an ancient civilization.
- Remember that one task can overlap many subject specific objectives; therefore, be sure to include all the various disciplines that apply.
- Create a checklist including the expectations of this task.
- Balance the checklist to ensure it covers essential skills for the task but does not overwhelm students and destroy the engagement created by the project.
- Share the checklist with students. Use this checklist as a form of student self-assessment for prior knowledge. What do they feel comfortable enough to share with others? What do they feel independently successful at? What would they like more instruction on?
- Use the completed checklist as an aid to deciding what expectations to cover as a class, what can be done in small groups, and who can be an expert assistant to others who might be struggling.
- Refer back to the checklist as the project evolves to ensure that students are using the needed skills in an accurate manner. Provide mini-lessons if gaps in knowledge appear.
- Use the checklist as a form of final assessment. Have the students use a different color to mark their comfort level at the end of the project.
- Use this same checklist as a tool for adding your own comments and thoughts.

CLOSURE

Engagement is higher when we use a task selected by the students to demonstrate knowledge. This engagement will lead to mastery; we can use this engagement to direct some of the mastery. By outlining the required skills, presenting them up front, and then reflecting on them at a later point, we make the skills part of the task. The mastery the students are striving to achieve will also let you check some of your curriculum objectives off the list in an empowering and engaging way.

6

Fostering the Creative Mindset

Creativity now is as important in education as literacy, and we should treat it with the same status.

— Ken Robinson, *TED Talk* (2006)

We all have the capacity to be creative thinkers. Watch a group of small children playing independently and you will quickly see that we are born with the power to be creative. The three-year-old's drawing, which may look like a scribble to the undiscerning eye, is described as "an alien monster attacking a marshmallow." Sadly, by the time the same child hits Grade 5, he or she will likely have identified him- or herself as "unimaginative" and will see only a scribble in the previous artwork. So what happened to the creatively confident three-year-old who evolved into the "I can't draw" ten-year-old? According to creativity expert Sir Ken Robinson, the way our schools are designed is squashing the creativity of our students. With the heavy focus on improving test scores, increasing literacy rates, and cutting budgets, school programs have little space for student autonomy and exploration. Leading educational experts, as well as policy makers, are beginning to advocate for the need to foster creativity within our students. As teachers, what can we do to create a classroom that cultivates creative thought?

First we need to reassess what it means to be creative. Once used to describe one's aptitude in the arts, "creativity" can no longer be seen as an innate gift. McWilliam (2009) described a shift in creativity from arts-based, singularized, and innate to a concept that is teachable, learnable, and assessable. We all have the capacity for creative thinking: generating and expanding ideas, considering hypotheses, infusing imagination, and searching for innovative outcomes in any activity. Creativity means generating outcomes that are original and have value. Judging originality can be done in relation to one's previous experience, to a group, or to entirely original circumstances. Creative thinking also requires judgment; i.e., our ability to judge the value of ideas created by ourselves and others.

But how often in our classrooms do we encourage students to come up with their own original ideas? And if we do, are these valued?

Student-driven learning fosters creativity as it provides a framework not in which only are students are not only encouraged to create their own ideas, but where the creation of these ideas are essential to the program. The ideas are inherently valuable to the individual students, as it is through their own curiosity that these ideas form.

"Curiosity about life in all of its aspects, I think, is still the secret of great creative people."
— Leo Burnett, advertising executive

Defining Creativity for Students

There are many aspects to creating the classroom environment itself that will support student-driven learning. One important element is ensuring that students feel the liberty and confidence to develop and find value in their own ideas. From the first day forward, we need to create a classroom where students celebrate their originality. Through the fostering of their creative-thinking skills, students will gain the motivation to explore their learning independently.

We must encourage younger students to retain the creative confidence we are all born with. From the first day of school onward, make creativity one of the learning attributes you espouse in the classroom. Most little ones know that they need to be good listeners, cooperative, caring, etc.; however, how often do they think of creativity as something everyone in the classroom needs to be mindful of, support, and celebrate? Making "creative thinking" one of your catch phrases will help students see examples of creativity and originality.

Older students have likely been in learning environments where they and the teachers have identified certain individuals as creative. Help older students reshape their understanding of what it means to be creative. Like any process, this requires development and training. Likening creativity to skill-development, such as improving your hockey game, might help them visualize creativity as something that is attainable by all.

The best way to define creativity in our classrooms might well be to increase the creativity in ourselves. As teachers we need to believe in our own ability to be creative practitioners. If we are asking for creativity from our students, we must develop our own creative-thinking processes. While we might not all play the piano, draw cartoons, or host sing-alongs in our classrooms, we all have the capacity to be creative teachers. Creativity is about seeking innovation within your practice. It is about pursuing alternatives for routines that, while functional, do little to support and foster student engagement. To encourage our own sense of creativity, we need to delve into the rather uncomfortable spot where we reflect on our own professional habits. What are you currently doing in your practice that you find boring? What do you dread doing? Can you find new ways to do achieve the same outcome? The very act of opening ourselves up to new ideas in our practice helps to spark creativity. Being prepared for a little chaos and discomfort as part of the process is just a natural side effect of igniting the spark!

Classroom Engagement to Cultivate a Creative Mind

How do we create an atmosphere in which our students feel safe to create and explore? How do we create an environment where our students come up with original ideas? And how do we get our students to extend themselves creatively?

It may seem obvious, but it must be said: people will take risks when they feel safe to fail, safe to be themselves. Celebrate and cultivate the wacky ideas in the classroom; provide examples of unusual choices made by artists, athletes, scientists, designers, etc. to give value to those who think differently. Advertising can be an incredible source of motivation for students to see different individuals who refused to follow the status quo. Both Apple and Nike have made a point of celebrating both the failures and successes of many famous individuals. Advertising found online and commercials on TV can provide inspirational modelling

TED, a nonprofit organization that works with leaders in Technology, Entertainment, and Design, hosts talks that "spread ideas worth sharing" on a wide variety of current issues. You can find a TED talk that will speak to your class about creativity, imagination, and the power of good ideas. See https://www.ted.com/talks

for those students who are held back by their desire to stay safe within the status quo.

Here is a list of ideas to inspire creative flow and risk-taking in the classroom:

- Use verbal and visual cues during classroom conversations and explorations to provide students with modelling of creative thought.
- Encourage and remain positive about different viewpoints and ideas.
- Encourage students to be prolific; aspiring to quantity can make it easier to find a quality idea.
- When students present an idea, challenge them to extend it further. For example, when presented with the idea of an airplane that can carry houses, challenge the idea: *What do you need to do to a regular airplane to handle the weight?*
- Base rules, such as disallowing the drawing of stick people, can force a higher level of creative thought. Note that such rules must be carefully applied only once you know and understand the abilities of your students.
- Never let students stop at the first idea. It is always a struggle to get beyond the first idea, often the one that appears to be the best and the easiest to achieve. Whenever possible, ask students to find at least two options for every idea.
- Follow the dictum of American composer John Cage: Begin anywhere. If a problem is stifling a child, encourage that student to delve into the middle or start at the end. Just begin.
- Group students in various ways. Diverse grouping of students is essential to fostering creativity. Allowing students to always find the same partners or always placing them in the same groups means they are never exposed to different ideas and viewpoints.
- Develop a "just leave it" mentality when students are frustrated or stuck. Encourage them to pursue a completely different task that will allow them to refocus their energies.
- Allow for doodling and fidgeting. Many individuals need to move to stimulate the creative process.
- Always look at a problem from more than one perspective. With younger students, this might mean physically moving a chair or desk to see something new; for older students, it could be probing them with questions about different viewpoints associated to a problem.
- Bring dissimilar objects and ideas together to encourage diverse thinking. For example, if your students are creating a time machine, provide them with different objects (a banana, a telephone, a wallet) and ask them how the objects could serve as time machines.

DETOUR: BRAINSTORMING

One tool used commonly in our classrooms to collect creative ideas is brainstorming. Often heralded as the opportunity to develop creative thinking in a group, it has limitations when used as the only method to generate ideas. Asking students to brainstorm encourages them to find as many possible outcomes for a problem or idea as they can. But if students are uninformed, brainstorming can result in the sharing of misinformation. Instead of feeling inspired by the collaboration of ideas, students can feel discouraged or frustrated by their lack of understanding or, worse, they can lose focus on the topic altogether.

For brainstorming to be effective for your students, consider the following guidelines:

- Remember that brainstorming is just one tool to help generate alternative ideas; it is not the only method of generating ideas.
- Identify a specific purpose for the brainstorm prior to beginning the activity.
- Limit the number of ideas that students are required to generate during a brainstorm. A reasonable goal is 30 to 50 ideas, as this number will give any student a large pool of possibilities.
- Brainstorming should be without judgment (no positive or negative feedback should be part of the process); otherwise, students might generate only ideas related to those that have received positive feedback.
- Encourage students to look for ways to combine or join their ideas when brainstorming. These combinations can inspire new alternatives.

Adapted from Treffinger et al (1998)

How to Build a Creative Classroom

> "The most creative spaces are those which hurl us together. It is the human friction that makes the sparks."
> — Jonah Lehrer, *Imagine* (2012)

While creative thinking is an internal process, it can be either inspired or stifled by the outside environment. Few of us can create in complete isolation; we need the inspiration of others and/or the inspiration of outside stimuli (posters, texts, digital technologies, music, movies, etc.). Students need an environment where they have space to explore, share, and pursue their own ideas.

Many big companies have invested considerable amounts of energy into creating spaces where workers are engaged and inspired. Steve Jobs, founder of Apple, understood the importance of a workspace that allowed (even insisted on) communication among peers. Why should our classrooms be any different? It is rare to enter a classroom and see desks in perfectly neat rows, isolated from each other and all facing the front of the room. This design, totally functional for a teacher-focused classroom, does little to encourage creative thinking.

We need to create a classroom community that physically and emotionally supports the creation of new ideas and fosters questions. This environment might cause some discomfort for students and it will certainly not always be harmonious. Some of our best ideas emerge through a little friction with others. To have ideas challenged puts people in a place where they need to defend their thoughts and work to clarify or correct areas that are not clear. In a classroom, teachers have a crucial role in providing modelling and monitoring to ensure that these conversations are not detrimental to the learning of the students.

Small Hop: Forming Classroom Agreements

DESTINATION

To create classroom agreements at the start of the year. These agreements will help provide a framework for the way the classroom will function as a community.

SHIFT

No first day of school is complete without a discussion of classroom expectations. Older students can parrot off class rules with little pause. But who sets these rules? And for what purpose? Allowing students to help identify what they need in a classroom invites them to take ownership of the classroom and their behavior within the class community.

SPARK

This classroom is a community of learners. What do you need to help you learn? What kind of classroom would you like to be a part of?

UNFOLDING THE ROADMAP

- Ask students to write (or draw) on sticky notes words that reflect their ideal classroom. Nudge students toward using broad terms rather than very specific ideas; e.g., "shares classroom materials equally" not "will give you an eraser." Younger children can gather these ideas as a group.
- Explain to students that the class is going to work together to create a set of agreements that will govern the classroom for the year. Everyone in the class will need to agree on the ideas. At this point, some students might want to reflect on their sticky notes.
- Ask students to stick their sticky notes to their desks/tables. If they have any that they do not want to share with their peers, they can pass them along to you. Students share their sticky notes in small groups of two or three individuals. Ask students to try to work together to group their ideas; e.g., suggest a category for "Really cool, but probably not realistic" ideas. Students will keep these groups together in individual piles. After a few minutes of discussion, ask students to pair up groups to make larger groups. They will need to group their sticky-note piles.
- Gather as a class and group the sticky-note piles. Tell students that they need to choose no more than ten ideas to be part of the list of agreements. Sort sticky-note groups (and outliers that did not fit into a group) into a class value line that ranges from "We really need this agreement" to "Our class could function without this agreement." Get consensus from all the students.
- Polish the final classroom agreements so that anyone could understand the ideas. Write out the classroom agreements and hang them in a prominent spot in the classroom.

CLOSURE

Your class agreements should not be gathering dust on the wall. At the start of the year, make a point of referring students to these agreements when they need direction. Remember that the agreements are not static and can be changed and reevaluated as needed throughout the year.

Make Creative Spaces in the Classroom

Collaboration does bring creativity, but few students benefit from being collaborative all the time. We all need spaces where we can quietly pursue our own ideas without interruption and interference by others. It is essential to provide a classroom where students have spaces for collaboration alongside spaces for quiet independent work. Few of us have the luxury of unlimited space in our classrooms, so we need to do some thoughtful organization to ensure that all students will have a workspace that can be both collaborative and solitary: discarded binders can make screens for those times when students want to work independently; cardboard display boards cut in half make excellent desk dividers.

If possible, try to build quiet time into each new activity or task. Allow your students to be comfortable in the quiet while they work on their ideas. For some, it might feel uncomfortable at first to not be able to constantly bounce their ideas around with their peers. But these students need quiet contemplation time where they can work on developing their own original ideas without being influenced by others.

Rethink how you have used the furniture in your classroom. Most of us try to organize our students into groups of two or more. These spaces obviously lend themselves to collaboration. But we also need to provide spaces that are comfortable and engaging. Sitting upright in a desk does not always inspire the creativity to flow!

Consider the following questions when designing your classroom:

- Are there areas in the classroom you could use to make informal discussion pits?
- When asked to work independently in the classroom, where do students all rush to? Piles of pillows are popular places for impromptu conversations.
- Do you have any furniture, such as large bookshelves or trolleys, that can be removed to make for more open space? Ideally, you want to provide space between the different areas within your classroom. These open spaces often become conversation corridors, where students are likely to stop and interact.
- How have you organized your digital tools? If you have computers and/or an interactive whiteboard, are these accessible to larger groups of students?
- What about your own workspace? Is it available and open for students? Can you work independently in your own classroom? Is it a space that you find inspiring?

Take time to consider the physical environment of your classroom. How and where can you make changes that will allow for greater collaboration as well as solitude?

POSTCARD FROM THE CLASSROOM

For many years, I had a large cumbersome teacher's desk. It had many drawers (crammed with elastic bands, confiscated toys, random pencils, sticky notes) and was stacked with student work. I hated that desk. I dreaded sitting down to review my students' work and, even more, I disliked that I never was able to sit and chat with my students around my workspace. After visiting some schools in inner-city Chicago, I was struck by the absence of the traditional teacher's desk. Some teachers had no workspace of their own, while others used simple drafting tables. Inspired, I returned to my school and dragged that heavy wooden obstacle out of my classroom. In its place I put a simple pine table. No drawers, no shelves, no hiding spots. I rescued some colorful boxes from a rummage sale and used these to store my elastic bands, rogue erasers, and such. Suddenly the feel of the classroom environment shifted. I no longer felt trapped by my workspace. Sitting down at my desk became a pleasure, and my students noticed the change immediately. My table became a conference centre, a favored reading spot, and an idea area in the classroom. Making that small change, from the traditional desk to a bare table, enabled me to find a welcoming spot for creative thinking.

Visuals Foster the Creative Process

We all respond to visual cues. A walk through an art gallery will elicit many different emotions, but few of them will be feelings of indifference. A classroom that encourages student-driven learning needs to consider the role of visual cues in supporting student thought processes and inspiring their ideas. When visuals are used mindfully, viewing a single image can be as powerful as reading an entire text or participating in a lengthy class discussion.

When you sit at a student's desk or table, what do you see from that perspective? When I first began teaching, I filled every inch of my classroom with posters, pictures, and photos. At the time, I thought the students would be visually engaged with all the stimuli. Over time, I realized that my efforts to stay true to the power of an image had created a visual cacophony.

We are fortunate to have many companies devoted to supplying teachers with resources. No matter what the subject, you can find posters, borders, and labels that relate to your topic. Often ordering these items takes just a simple click on the computer, and you can have a box delivered to you filled with theme-related visuals for your classroom. But these pre-packaged visuals aren't always what they seem; while they might provide a more professional appearance to your classroom, they do very little to foster creativity and student ownership. A classroom full of student-created posters, although not shiny, is one that is constantly being accessed and referred to. It is a space that speaks of student involvement and proudly displays their knowledge.

Small Hop: Creating Classroom Visuals

DESTINATION

From the start of the year, allow your students to create visuals for the classroom. These visuals can be instructive, directive, or purely for inspiration.

SHIFT

Move away from using your own visuals (either bought or made by you or bought). Allow your students to help take ownership of what visuals are needed and how these visuals are constructed.

SPARK

Blank walls need to be filled. That alone creates endless possibilities.

UNFOLDING THE ROADMAP

- Begin by leaving some or all of your bulletin boards blank. Trust your students to find ways to fill the space. Have a class conversation about appearances and what work will best represent the classroom. Allow students to decide what types of bulletin-board spaces they want to include in the classroom; e.g., writer's wall, math centre, posting for local news or interests.
- Teach and model how to create a poster. What criteria are involved? What is the purpose? What visual effects would you add? To experiment with the concept of poster-making, students can design posters to explain concepts to each other; we can use poster-making as a tool for students to teach each other concepts.

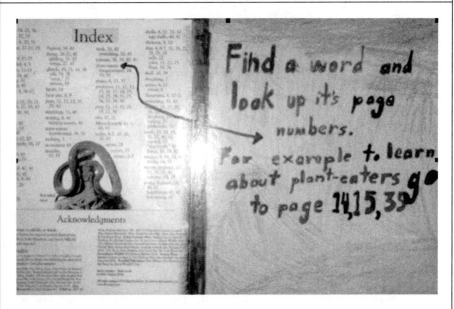

Ms. Crippin used poster-making as a resource tool for her Grade 3 students to share their strategies for reading nonfiction texts. They loved it and were eager to share their posters with peers. Rather than a being a space that the students could ignore, the class posters made the classroom walls tools that the students were proud to reference.

- Provide wall space that is entirely the students' to own. They can add or post what they like. You might cover this space with butcher paper so the wall becomes the art or learning area. Or you can provide students with tape and staples to add as they would like. This space can be a place for them to post pictures or words that describe themselves. It could also be a large mind map of what they are learning.
- Encourage students to bring in inspirational quotes and artwork to add to the classroom. Take time to talk about what makes a visual eye-catching; create a list together that will serve to help eager students remember the class's ideas of what they want to see on their walls.
- With younger children who are just beginning to print, trace or create bubble letters that the students can color in themselves. As students' skills progress, replace these signs with ones that they have created independently. Younger children can also
  - create the letters of the alphabet or a number line that will be referenced to throughout the year
  - write out labels for parts of the classroom and classroom supplies
  - add their own words to the class word wall
  - create posters of math concepts
  - become the Sign-maker, a rotating job that students create for their classroom, ensuring that the classroom displays are never static

CLOSURE

What if a student's poster has a spelling mistake or is not as we would have made it? We need to ask ourselves the important questions: Is the concept covered?

Is the poster effective for the concept it is covering? Does the mistake affect the learning of the concept? If the answer to this last question is yes, the concept needs to be reviewed and the poster corrected. For instance, if students confused subject and predicate in their parts of a sentence or if they cannot show that addition increases the size of a sum, then the concept was not understood and needs to be reviewed. If the mistake is not related to the concept, then leave it. For instance, if the sentence is "The kiten is black." and the poster is about complete sentences, then leave it. This poster will serve its purpose for the students. The author of the word "kiten" might at a later point realize the error and seek to correct it. If not, it can be addressed when double consonants are taught at a later point in the year. Learning evolves and our students need to experience that evolution naturally, rather than having us provide the end result.

Visual Literacy

If you have access to the technology in your classroom, photo-manipulation applications can provide students with digital tools that can extend their vision tremendously.

Choosing to share with students a few powerful images that change often might be more powerful for sparking discussion and inspiration than a bank of pictures that remain on the walls all year. Encourage students to bring in their own powerful images to add to the classroom. Reinforce the idea that a powerful image needs to evoke strong emotion and questions, but it cannot be offensive or disturbing to anyone in the classroom. For older students, the discussion of what images are appropriate for the classroom can definitely prompt compelling thoughts and questions.

Before embarking on any discussions around visual literacies, it is important to establish guidelines around personal perception. We all see what we want to see. As with any kind of literacy, our perceptions can be swayed by cultural, social, and personal influences. When discussing an image without any background information, we must be mindful to allow students to share their ideas openly without encouraging or discouraging certain assumptions. Until we have done some investigation, there can be no "correct" or "incorrect" observation— everyone can share their own opinions and viewpoints. Once some background has been provided, it continues to be important to validate different ideas and not allow celebration among those students who were "right" in their assumptions over those who saw something else.

POSTCARD FROM THE CLASSROOM

One teacher I know hung a picture frame at the front of the classroom and used it as a space for a rotating gallery of student-selected images. At the start of each week, students spent time discussing and debating the images. Some students chose well-known artworks, others chose photographs of current events, and some decided to draw their own pictures. Occasionally the teacher would ask students to find images related to their curriculum, while at other times she left the decisions open to the students. As the year progressed, the image changed often, as students clamored to be the ones to share their powerful picture with their peers.

For more on formative and summative assessment, see The Learning Map (pages 104, 109).

Medium-sized Drive: Reading Pictures

DESTINATION

To provide students with literacy skills to critically decode images. This is an excellent frontloading activity to spark student interest at the start of the unit, or it can be used as a formative or summative assessment to observe what students have gleaned from their research.

SHIFT

Thanks to advances in digital technologies, there are few spaces in our world where we are not being bombarded with images from media. We need to become savvy at reading these pictures: i.e., looking for clues in the images, drawing connections between pictures, and considering different perspectives associated with each image. Helping students become critical readers of visual literacies will provide them with an advantage as our world continues to move away from traditional texts.

SPARK

Ask "How do we read pictures?"

UNFOLDING THE ROADMAP

- Choose a compelling image from a current event or from the past that relates to a topic of study the students are familiar with. An image that focuses on a scene, rather than a close-up, might be easier to use to begin a discussion. For example, showing a close-up of a bird covered in oil will not generate many questions in a Grade 3 class, but choosing an image of an oil-covered bird at the edge of a tar pond brings into context several questions and issues.
- Provide several copies of the picture (as a digital image or in paper copies) or project it on an interactive whiteboard or wall where all students can visually access it.
- Familiarize yourself with background information so you can prompt the discussion to delve a little deeper. As well, have resources available so that students can search for the answers to their questions independently.
- Allow students several moments to observe the image without talking. It is difficult to refocus enthusiasm once conversation gets going, and it is important that all students have a chance to make note of what they first observe in the image.
- Without discussion, allow each student to make one observation about the image. I like the model in which each student stands quietly and shares his or her idea and then sits down (known as Stand and Deliver), so that all students can hear each others' observations and get a chance to contribute.
- After recording and/or listening to all observations, prompt students to fill in any gaps. Did they consider the *who, what, where, when,* and *why* in their observations?
- Probe deeper by asking students to explain their observations; e.g., *Why do you think the image is taken in Canada and not another country?*
- Now allow students time to ask questions about the image. These questions can serve as the beginnings of a research project or an introduction to a science or history lesson. Or they might simply be questions, and interested students can pursue the answers independently.

Taking time to build students' visual literacy provides them with new sources of information. Often a compelling photo, painting, or drawing will create more idea sparks then a well-written text, and it is a quick way to engage all students in a topic.

In today's world of visual media, it is not difficult to find compelling images. The following sites have beautifully constructed thought-provoking pictures:

- http://www.theselby.com/
- http://www.pictorymag.com/
- http://totallycoolpix.com/
- http://photography.nationalgeographic.com/photography/
- http://www.thephotoargus.com/

POSTCARD FROM THE CLASSROOM

For Ms. Fleming's Grade 2 unit on the pond, students chose to create accurate diagrams of their pond animals as a visual reference.

How to Assess Creativity in Our Students

"Creativity is so delicate a flower that praise tends to make it bloom while discouragement often nips it at the bud."
— Alex Osborn, quoted in Lehrer (2002)

Creativity, as a skill, can be difficult to perceive within ourselves. Who determines what ideas are valuable and what ideas are not? A quick look into history shows many examples of individuals whose ideas were disregarded as nonsensical or completely irrelevant, but later went on to shape some part of our common history (otherwise we might still think the world was flat!). As educators, how do we keep from applying our own biases to our students' ideas? More importantly, how do we foster the creative process at the same time as fulfilling our obligations to evaluate and assess our students' work and understanding? There is a need to assess creativity to help our students see where they are and to help guide them to the next steps. Assessment allows our students the opportunity to move forward, expand what they are currently doing, and ultimately critically think about what they learn.

When assessing creativity in the work of your students, it is critical to ascribe a specific definition of creativity in the context of the students and curriculum standards. As an educator, you need to establish this definition prior to assessment. Creativity might include

- an imaginative and playful approach
- questioning and making connections to other things, people, events, objects
- a willingness to take risks and experiment while learning
- discovering many possible solutions to a problem
- using a variety of elements, objects, and tools to express thought

Our students are a critical element of assessment and it is necessary to include them in the assessment process. Making our students active participants in assessment makes them critically reflective, as they are trying to adhere not only to our definition of creativity, but also to their own beliefs.

Some researchers and educators advocate using the following criteria as benchmarks for assessing creativity in the classroom:

Fluency: The number of different ideas produced.

Elaboration: Richness of detail in the ideas produced.

Flexibility: The number of categories of ideas that are produced.

Originality: The uniqueness of the ideas produced.

Within the creative context, we need to also think about our students as

- Confident: They enjoy the independence of creating; they are engaged, focused, and self-motivated while creating.
- Collaborative: They communicate with their peers and teachers to persevere though challenges; they listen to others and think about their own perspectives to find a creative solution they are satisfied with.
- Skilful: They can organize, plan, and manage their creative process with a solid vision.
- Knowledgeable: They are aware of different types of creative forms, styles, and artistic impressions and can use these techniques to expand their understanding.
- Reflective: They use assessment, dialogue, and collaboration to further refine their own creative process.

Adapted from Sue Ellis, "Creative Learning Assessment" (2009)

For more on formative and summative assessment, see The Learning Map (page 109).

7

Diving into a Deeper Understanding

Arriving at one goal is the starting point to another.
— John Dewey, *How We Think* (1910)

Everything we do—from getting to know our students, through putting our students in the driver's seat, to pushing for intrinsic motivation and building creative confidence—is a foundation for fostering deeper understanding in our students. We want our students to be immersed in their learning so that they

- Ask meaningful questions
- Connect information from one context to another
- Evaluate and judge information as it is relevant to their lives
- Understand various perspectives and how they might influence their understanding
- Delve deeper into areas of interest
- Take action on their learning in a meaningful context

Engagement is key. Once we have our students engaged in learning, they naturally drive right off the set course into different routes. They are on a mission; we are sitting in the passenger seat, offering suggestions and giving advice. Occasionally we might insist that they stop and ask for directions, but more often we are smiling with sheer pleasure as they take control. We want our students to be engaged in their learning so they can move past fact-gaining missions and drive into thinking critically.

Critical Thinking

Critical thinking is a fantastic term and one that most people believe in. Everyone wants their students to think critically. But what does that mean? How does that translate into our classrooms? How do we teach it? And how do we know when our students have achieved it?

Critical thinking…

"…[is the] active, persistent, and careful consideration of any belief or supposed form of knowledge in the light of the grounds that support it and the further conclusions to which it tends." — John Dewey (1910)

"…[is] the thinking through of a problematic situation about what to believe or how to act where the thinker makes a reasoned judgment that reflects competent use of the intellectual tools for quality thinking." — The Thinking Consortium

The Thinking Consortium 2 (at www.tc2.ca) has many resources and ideas for embedding critical thought into the classroom.

"…calls for a persistent effort to examine any belief or supposed form of knowledge in the light of the evidence that supports it and the further conclusions to which it tends." — Edward Glaser (1941)

What do all of these definitions have in common? Critical thinking is

- evaluating information
- extracting meaning
- making a decision

Critical thinking takes a plethora of ideas and distills them into one big idea. We evaluate what we have, analyzing, questioning, coming from different perspectives; we extract meaning from it; and then we make a decision. It is an ongoing process that we are constantly involved in. Getting our students to think creatively engenders many ideas; however, now how do we analyze them to ensure that the idea meets our learning goal?

Once we have the idea, we need to go back to evaluate it:

Does it work? Is there a better alternative?
Will this work for me?
What can I use. What will not work?

If you are reading this book, you too are engaged in critical thinking about how you can change your teaching practice.

Testing it, modifying it, and then changing it is what keeps us engaged.

The key to critical thinking is to make it a vibrant part of the classroom dynamic so that it becomes expected and assumed. It cannot happen only after a unit or each Friday at 10:00. It is alive in the daily activities. Creative thinking is the gasoline that helps drive the students in their learning.

Medium-sized Drive: Finding the Big Idea

DESTINATION

Recognizing the key idea(s) that students will need to take away from a unit.

SHIFT

We no longer expect our students to memorize and retain a series of facts around a unit or concept. But for our students to be able to make future connections to other units or concepts, they all need to finish the unit and have the same essential understandings. In a classroom that uses student-driven learning, helping students to recognize the big idea prior to beginning a task allows a more open-ended approach to coming to those essential understandings. For example, if it is required that all students learn about ancient civilizations, the big idea might be *All ancient civilizations had a form of trade, language, etc.* Rather than focusing the unit tightly on the Mayans, students can explore a civilization of their choice, as long as they ensure they can support the big idea with examples and facts.

SPARK

Engage your students to create. Ask them, *In one or two sentences, what do you think everyone needs to know when they finish this unit?*

- Finding the big idea is not a process you begin a unit with; rather it is a process you start with your students once they have completed the frontloading and are familiar with the required curriculum objectives.
- Prior to beginning the task, remind students that just one fact about the topic will not tell us all we need to know.
- Ask students to write one or two sentences that could possibly describe the unit. Share the sentences; they will likely be specific fact-based statements. Go through the different statements, asking students to look for similarities among them. Verbs that stand out, nouns that are repeated—these words can help identify a pattern in what information stands out during the frontloading process. With younger children, you might have them find a picture that represents what the unit could be about.
- Begin to guide students toward creating a single statement about the unit. Encourage them to make a broad statement, one that could work for many different parts of the unit and is not specific to one area. With older students, you might allow them to work in small groups to try to create their own statement.
- Write the examples of the big idea in a visible spot in the classroom. I have found sentence-strip papers excellent for writing out big ideas.

CLOSURE

As students continue in their learning, revisit the big ideas; challenge students to distill the various statements into one singular statement that represents the unit. As you work together with your students to prepare the assessment of their learning, return to the big idea. What pieces of information do they need to know to be able to prove that statement is true? For smaller units, they might be able to cite one or two examples to support the big idea; that could be your summative assessment. Don't discard the big ideas as you move on different units and topics; as the year progresses, remind the students of the various big ideas they have formed. Encourage them to look for connections to other topics and areas of interest.

Gathering Information

Provide Structure

To teach our students to think critically, we need to begin by providing a framework they can use. When we teach a multiplication problem, we often give students more than one method to use. We want them to pick a way that works best for their learning. When helping students think critically, we also need to provide them with alternatives.

Breaking the process into steps helps form an outline as you begin and makes the process more tangible for some learners. But stepping back and allowing students to select what might work for them or modifying the plan are equally essential. Here are a few frameworks that you might decide to go with:

FRAMEWORK A

1. Identify purpose or goal.
2. Create a critical question about the goal.

All frameworks are cyclical; we need to bring students back with their end result in their hand. When they evaluate it, do they like the outcome? Do they need to go back to alter it?

3. Assemble the relevant data.
4. Evaluate different points of view.
5. Identify the most viable options.
6. Determine which you will move forward with.
7. Evaluate the decision: Did it work?

FRAMEWORK B

1. Determine the purpose.
2. From the purpose, create a problem or question to solve.
3. List possible assumptions that might impede your perspective.
4. Clarify your point of view.
5. Collect data, information, and evidence.
6. Sort and represent data, information, and evidence in charts and visuals.
7. Critique the information.
8. Draw a conclusion.
9. Evaluate the implications and consequences of the conclusion.

Begin the Process of Critical Questioning

In order for students to ask critical questions, we need to provide background. We need to teach them how to think critically, in a visible and intentional way, so they understand what we are asking. And we need to use their areas of knowledge or provide them with sufficient knowledge to push their understanding, and ours, to the next level.

Being visible about our thought process means that we are explicitly modelling how to think. We are changing the flow of education from being about memorizing facts to being about creating ideas and we are explicitly teaching how to generate and work through those ideas. We are taking the hood off the car and sharing what happens in the engine so students can solve their own problems. Of course, our students are already thinking. But we want to show them how to dive a bit deeper into their flow of thought before jumping to the next idea.

POSTCARD FROM THE CLASSROOM

For our unit on structures, we contacted teacher Heather Love in Thailand for an online video conference. She walked us around their street and showed us what their structures look like. Ms. Love generously offered to hold her laptop while walking in Bangkok and chatting with my students. I turned off the lights and projected the phone call on the interactive whiteboard. What first struck my young students was the darkness. Why was it afternoon here and night-time there? We had a rich conversation about the sun and the earth's movement. Opening up the world with digital media created many authentic and rich conversations about the earth, structures, and culture that led us into the weeks ahead.

Think Aloud

When we talk through what we are doing as we are doing it, we are modelling how to think. In a verbal way, we are breaking up the problem into a flow and sharing it with our students. Luckily, the invention of the cell phone has made people talking to themselves socially acceptable. So let's run with it. We might sound like this: "I was hoping to create more space in this area of the room for group work, but I am not too sure how to arrange the furniture. I could push…"; or "This math question seems tricky. I am stopped up by the fact that it has several digits, but if I look at it this way I could break it down. Or I could break it down this way…. Does anyone else have a suggestion?"; or "I can see that George is upset. I know that he thinks I caused the problem, but I don't know what I did. I will ask him and see if I can comfort him." When we think aloud, we give kids the opportunity to see what is happening inside our heads prior to a decision or idea becoming action; it makes the process more visible. It feels odd at first, but you (and your students) will quickly adapt, and you might find yourself in public at the grocery store vocalizing your choices for dinner that night.

POSTCARD FROM THE CLASSROOM

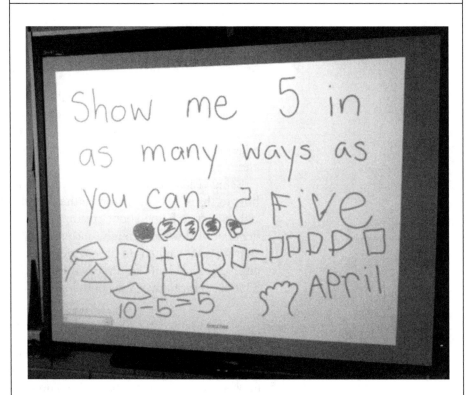

In Christina Morgan-Poort's Grade 1/2 split, students explored different ways to find five. Their inventiveness extended far beyond the traditional numeracy lesson.

Big Journey: Sorting Our Thinking

DESTINATION

To help our students become aware of the types of thoughts or ideas they are having.

SHIFT

Each classroom has moments throughout the day when topics are discussed. Often ideas are shared and brought together. In an effort to help our students share a range of ideas and perspectives, we can help them be more visible about the type of ideas they are presenting.

SPARK

Use any class discussion or topic, such as "Which do you think is better: local or imported food?"

UNFOLDING THE ROADMAP

- Create a variety of manipulatives for thinking. In our classroom, thinking sticks are craft sticks with an idea written on each. Ideas on thinking sticks can include
  Facts: ideas that share data, facts, or knowledge about the topic
  Feelings: ideas that share feelings or emotions about the topic
  Values: ideas that share values and help to explain why something may or may not work
  Connections: ideas that connect to other ideas and build on what we know
  Causations: ideas that link to what might happen next if we keep building in a certain direction
  Creativity: ideas that offer a new idea or solution for the topic
  Plans: ideas that connect to other ideas and put them into a time plan, sequence, or structure
- The thinking perspectives can shift and change, depending on whether they are introduced gradually or all at once, and on when they apply to the topic area.
- At some point prior to beginning the discussion, introduce the thinking sticks. Let students know that they are used for both sharing their ideas and asking questions.
- As students share ideas, ask if they can identify which stick they are using.
- Posting the types of sticks on a chart or interactive whiteboard allows students to easily track their ideas and questions with tally marks or checks. This also shows what sticks are not being used, or what perspectives we might be missing in our talk.

CLOSURE

When students are made more aware of their ideas, the conversation becomes more balanced by multiple perspectives. Students are thinking of which perspective they are using and which ones they tend to rely on. They are also trying to balance perspectives naturally and add in ones that are not yet in play. They are thinking of multiple perspectives.

Provoke Some Thought

One parent and her four-year old curator post daily videos to the site The Kid Should See This at http://thekidshouldseethis.com/. These videos are sure to inspire conversations in your classroom.

Asking our students to get engaged and dive deeper into their learning requires that we share the same passions. We need to engage in their learning to provoke thought. In provoking thought, we ask our students to think about an idea and then build on it. To elicit their first gut reaction, we can

- Ask questions that spark thought or controversy
- Show pictures or graphics that prompt discussion
- Do something out of routine that pushes questions

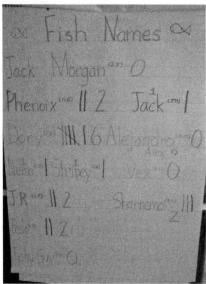

In Ms. Heyes' Senior Kindergarten class, the students were keen to name the class fish. There were many suggestions! To sort their ideas, they put names on the tank itself; afterward, these names were converted into a tally chart and finally a bar graph. In the end, this helped students organize their thinking.

Once we have captured our students' attention, we want them to spend time diving to that deeper level. We want them to think about their ideas and/or the question at hand to bring a rich conversation to the table. There are many ways to inspire our learners to extend their thinking on a topic:

- Provide students with time to form their responses. After asking a question, give a moment to let it sink in.
- Encourage a series of responses: *That is one idea, does anyone have anything to add?*
- Think–Pair–Share (Lyman, 1981): pose a question and give the students a chance to think, talk to a buddy, and then share their response.
- Put a time crunch on the discussion. Pose a question and give 60 seconds for the students to talk to each other, loudly and eagerly, to better form their ideas. Bring the class together and share.
- Write it out: Give students a piece of paper or a "ticket out the door," asking them what they learned. Use this to guide the next discussion and lesson.

- Take inventory: Pose a question and ask students to put their thumbs in the air. Pointing up means they have a response; down means they need assistance or time.

Unlock Vocabulary

Depending on what framework you use, you need to teach key vocabulary words to students so that they can move forward with these terms "in their pocket." It will be easier for students to think of and share ideas if they can access a variety of words that deepen their perspective. For instance, teaching the difference between estimation (using the clues around you to respond) and guessing (random response) lets us help our students understand the type of thinking process at work and what factors might be influencing their thoughts. Depending on the framework they are using and their age level, the vocabulary will differ. Possible key words might be

- *purpose, idea, goal*
- *guess, estimate, hypothesis, question, opinion*
- *critique, examine, interpret, research*
- *design, invent, experiment*
- *describe, paraphrase, demonstrate, summarize*
- *simplify, categorize, connect*
- *communicate, inform, participate, articulate*

Getting Ideas to Sink In

"Memory is the residue of thought."
— Daniel Willingham, *Why Don't Students Like School?* (2010)

We want our students to be deeply engaged in their learning. Clearly, this is not a new or unheard-of goal for any teacher. But how do we build the foundation for thinking when our students are thinking about an upcoming soccer game or music concert as the lesson dangles in front of their absent eyes? How do we ensure that our students are engaged? To sink learning into that valuable long-term memory pocket, students need to pay active attention to what they are learning. On our side, how do we engage that active learning? We need to

- Determine the one big idea that we clearly want our students to know.
- Form our lesson around the bit idea to reinforce the meaning.
- Carefully select our activities so that we are not adding distraction and taking away from the big idea.
- Repeat and review the big idea throughout the activity to build on students' learning.
- Connect the idea to their understanding, building on what has been previously covered.
- Have them ask questions about the big idea at points throughout the lesson.

Medium-sized Drive: Understanding Our Learning with Portfolios

DESTINATION

To engage our students in their learning with the use of portfolios. A student portfolio is a collection of work, usually sorted, that is reflected on as part of the learning process.

Traditionally student work is sorted into pockets or folders in a portfolio. Students are responsible for selecting and reflecting on a piece and putting it in the appropriate folder. The shift is in the folders' names. Rather than labelling the folders with the subject, change the titles of the folders to reflect more visible learning. Possible names for the folders include *Knowledge or Skill Activities*, *Critical Thought*, *Collaborating*, *Motivation*, etc. Or the folders can be based on different types of thinking models. Regardless of what model you select, this sorting technique will push students to think about their thinking when beginning and completing a task. It will change how they view their work and the process to complete it.

UNFOLDING THE ROADMAP

- Set up the portfolio experience: share with the students what tool, physical or digital, that they will be using to bank or store their work.
- Have students claim the portfolio: ask them what they would do with the cover that would best represent them as a learner.
- Prepare how students will divide up the portfolio, considering all the types of work that will be placed in it.
- Ask students what types of information should be put into the folder. As students provide examples of what should be placed in the folders, sort their list into the categories you are considering. For example:

• projects • gymnastic routines	• worksheets • math speed tests • spelling tests	• group work • literacy circles	• fun stuff
New Understandings	*Inquiry Work*	*Skill Work*	*Group Work*	*Motivating Work*

- Use concept attainment as a tool to allow students to create category titles for the groupings they listed. In the chart above, the second row shows possible titles.
- Add categories you think they might need that are not mentioned. I added one called New Understandings to the chart so that when the students discover something new or deepen their current understanding of a concept, they can add it here and track their learning.
- In this type of portfolio, all students are not going to place each item in the same pocket. Some might choose to include a piece that they feel passionate about and put it under Motivating Work, whereas another might select the same piece and put it under Inquiry Work. Being able to justify the placement is what is important. They are learning to gauge and sort their own learning.

CLOSURE

When we think of our learning in a visual way and teach our students different types of tasks, students become aware of the type of tasks they complete. This type of sorting can lead to comments like "Can we do more group work?" or "I really like inquiry" or "I am motivated when we do computer tasks." We, too, become more aware of the type of tasks we are designing. We can listen and use students' portfolio sorting as feedback for our teaching. What tasks are they drawn to? What do they put in the Skills or New Understandings folder? Did they grasp the concept of group work in a specific task?

Making a Decision

Games and Tricks for Deeper Diving

There are many games and tricks for getting students to think more critically about their learning. A quick Internet search turns up many spelling, competition, or collaborative activities. Here are a few of our favorite games and tricks, activities we use to get our students to choose a perspective on a topic or to explore a topic at a deeper level of understanding.

FOUR CORNERS

Place the words *Strongly agree*, *Agree*, *Disagree*, and *Strongly disagree* in the corners of the classroom. Present a statement; e.g., *Printing is no longer necessary*. Ask students to place themselves in the corner that matches how they feel.

ON THE LINE

Another debating technique, in which a statement is shared—e.g., *All ancient civilizations used technology for advancement*; *All students should wear uniforms*; or *Spiderman is a good friend*—and students need to gauge what they believe and place themselves on a line. At one end of the line is *Strongly agree* and at the other end is *Strongly disagree*. Once in position, students need to justify their decision. An opportunity to change where they are in line is useful to show changes in thinking, but they also need to justify why they are changing.

SO WHAT?

Choose an issue (such as global warming or the education of children) and brainstorm why that issue is important. For each idea, ask the question *So what?* again, and brainstorm why the sub-issue is important. In the end, you will have a large web of linking ideas, all supporting the initial idea as important.

FLIPPING IT

Take a solution (such as reducing fish farming or listening to friends before reacting) and find other problems that the solution might also solve.

CONNECT THE SPOTS

This pulls together the key words or ideas from the unit of study. Have students connect the words in a concept or mind map as a class, in groups, or individually. If this is done as a small-group activity, have the students share their responses and ideas with each other.

WRITING IN ROLE

What better way to get authentic writing than to create a dramatic atmosphere? Writing in role is a well-researched and discussed technique that involves students getting into the mindset of a character and then writing from that perspective. We have also used the interactive whiteboard to project complementary images and sound systems with dim lights to create mood for the dramatic reading; e.g., posting images of boats at sea and ocean noises to accompany writing about the early immigrant experience.

PERSPECTIVE DEBATE

Create a topic and a list of stakeholders in the topic; e.g., the topic of early Canadian aboriginal schooling, with aboriginal children, aboriginal parents, priests, government officials, European settlers as stakeholders. Once students have an understanding of the topic, give each a piece of paper with a character to play. Students must then speak on behalf of their characters for the discussion.

Big Journey: Making Connections

DESTINATION

Helping students shrink and expand their perspectives to include and connect to global and personal issues.

SHIFT

Often students learn information in isolation, without looking to see how it might connect to their own lives, without looking outward to see how it could connect to global issues; e.g., studying the destruction of the Amazon rainforest without identifying that there are rainforests in Canada and understanding how different lifestyle choices affect the destruction of these forests. When students learn in isolation, it severs any connections they could possibly make between issues. Understanding how to make connections between and among topics is an integral part of student-driven learning. A student who is passionate about arctic animals might want to spend the better part of the year studying up on the life of the polar bears. While we want to foster this interest and engagement, we need to make sure our students ask the essential questions about their topic: *Who cares?* and *So what?*

SPARK

Everything connects to something else—nothing can survive in isolation. Ask students to brainstorm issues connected to them that they feel are important. Share these issues as a class and look for common connections.

UNFOLDING THE ROADMAP

- Prior to a unit, or as a stand-alone activity, ask students to bring in current-event articles or send you links to Web articles relating to a given topic. For younger children, you might want to choose a few articles or images related to local issues they can connect with easily.
- Read or orally review one of the articles. An interactive whiteboard works very well for this activity, as you can ask the students to highlight the big ideas and supporting facts. With younger children, you could ask students to share their thoughts orally after they have been given a synopsis of the event.
- As a group, decide on the big idea of the event: *What is happening that is making the event newsworthy?*
- Write the big idea on the board or whiteboard.
- Ask students to come up with the different people who might care about the issue (individuals and groups): *Who cares?* You might want to create a web with the big idea in the middle and the people who care as spokes.

- After coming up with the different people who care about the event, challenge students to think about how these people might connect. You might get them to write these connections down.
- Look at the big idea and ask your students to reflect on the next question: *So what?* Have a class discussion on why this issue is important. Why do they feel people should care about this issue?
- If the class is engaged in the conversation, you might want to prompt them to guess why the different groups/individuals (the answers to *Who cares?*) might feel the issue is important.
- Keep a record of the conversation in hard copy, on the whiteboard, or even as a VoiceThread recording. As students delve more deeply into the topic at hand, they might find more connections to the big idea and brainstorm more ideas of why the issue is important.
- With older children who are working on current-events projects, challenge students by asking them to get together and find connections between their different topics. It is amazing what evolves from these kinds of conversations.

CLOSURE

This activity is formally structured, but it can easily be turned into a more casual conversation. While asking an enthusiastic student "Who cares about this topic?" might feel like dampening the student's spirit, it is a powerful way to help students realize how their own interests connect to the world and how global issues connect to them.

POSTCARD FROM THE CLASSROOM

ISSUE	WHY I CARE	WHO ELSE MIGHT CARE

In Grade 5 we used this simple template as part of our current-events discussions. Prior to bringing in an article to share with the class, students brainstormed the key issue and the stakeholders who might care about the issue.

DETOUR: HAVE WE GONE DEEP ENOUGH?

When the process of student-driven learning is at work, it can be an incredible thing. Our teaching practice is constantly changing with our students. We know our students and can see them using all of their creative powers, navigating their own ideas. They are motivated, engaged, and resilient when faced with challenges.

At this point in our journey, we all—students and teacher—need to pause and reflect. Are we headed in the right direction? Do we need further instruction? How can we show our learning map? Here are some important questions to consider:

- *Can I explain the issue?*

- *Do I know who/what is connected to my issue?* Can I identify who the stakeholders are related to my idea?
- *Is my idea transferable?* Can I apply my solution to other problems beyond the one I just solved?
- *Is my idea the best solution for the problem?* Does it create other problems/questions?
- *Can I prove the validity of my idea?* Do I have evidence or examples to support my opinions?
- *Does my solution positively or negatively influence other ideas?* Can I identify other perspectives related to my idea?
- *Is my idea credible?* Are my sources valid?
- *How can I teach other people my solution?* Are my ideas clear? Does my solution make sense to others?
- *Have I addressed the issue?* Have I met the criteria? Have I met my goals?

Assessment

For a more detailed discussion of assessment, see The Learning Map (page 103).

Assessment is a tricky word. For many teachers, an end-of-task unit assessment can become a driving force. Do our students know what we just taught them? Can they do A, B, and C? Will they meet the requirements of the next test? The focus is on the end result rather than on the process. We know that many more learning opportunities come from each task and assignment than can be represented by a check mark at the end of the piece. Assessment is an integral part of the classroom experience, but it is not the driving force.

The Power of Documentation

More than a project or a single task that a student completes, a solid summative assessment comes from the collection of information we have from our students. The growth of our students is apparent when we collect:

- Formative Assessment/Assessment for Learning: The work completed at the beginning of the unit along with students' questions that helps us remember their prior knowledge of the topic.
- Ongoing Assessment/Assessment as Learning: The activities and feedback (from peers, teachers, and self-reflection) that show a growth cycle while the topic is being studied.
- Summative Assessment/Assessment of Learning: The final piece(s) of work (drawings, descriptions, answers to questions, etc.) that show students' knowledge after the topic has been studied.

This combination of material creates a story of the learner throughout the unit of study. Their individual progress through their interests becomes apparent. What is covered in our classrooms extends beyond the snapshot of a standardized test; this collection of data shows the intricate detail and richness the student has absorbed. As well, this collection takes a large leap away from comparative assessment, in which each student completes the same task and students are ranked according to a skill level in a linear fashion.

8

The Learning Map

Everything growing wild is a hundred times stronger than tame things.

— Forrest Carter, *The Education of Little Tree*

Bringing student-driven learning into your classroom is a bit like following a hand-drawn map. There are odd little landmarks, such as deep student questions or a student overheard giving critical feedback to a peer, that hint you are headed in the right direction. But as with most hand-drawn maps, you need trust in the mapmaker and have faith that you will arrive at your destination. In this analogy, as teacher you are also the mapmaker—you need to set the course for establishing independence, innovation, and engagement in your classroom.

This book has discussed the elements of student-driven learning: shifting the focus of teaching practice; knowing our students; fostering creativity; fueling student learning; leaving the linear path; and knowing when and how to dig deeper into the curriculum. It has presented ideas of how you can bring these elements into your classroom; however, by themselves, these ideas are simply landmarks. In any new journey, one needs a map to know how to begin.

Student-driven learning does have structure, it does require assessment, and, as a practice, it needs constant reflection. This last chapter provides some ideas of how you can plan for and assess student-driven learning in your classrooms.

Two Principles of Assessment

Assessment with student-driven learning follows two unwritten principles. First, learning is cyclical; learning never dies. Just as our students (and we) never stop learning, neither does the process of thinking about what we have done, evaluating it, and trying to make it better ever end. Secondly, in student-driven learning it is imperative that the student be an integral partner in the process of assessment from the beginning.

Students must be involved in

- **Planning:** Engaging in determining how the task should be assessed. What is the curriculum objective being targeted? What other factors that can be assessed will be in play during the task?
- **Reflecting:** Using tools and thinking about their learning, their process, and what direction they need to take next to achieve their outcomes.

- **Designing:** Choosing assessment tools to be used. Creating a brief overview of assessment tools that might work will help students gain a solid understanding of the goal toward which they will be designing their project. With the task in mind, can they think of how best to demonstrate their knowledge? Create a list of criteria for a task that reflects the objectives. Ensure the criteria are flexible enough to allow for various types of projects.
- **Evaluating:** During and after the task, thinking of both the goals and their learning through the process. Are they driving in the wrong direction? Did they get diverted off the path? Will they be able to regain control or do we need to go in for a rescue?

Getting Trip-Ready

Assessment for Learning

As teachers, we sometimes find meeting the individual needs of our students daunting. Yet it is also a task we feel passionate about. We want to see our students succeed. We want to be the cheerleaders behind them, pushing them past their expectations. We want to help them move to their next step. Understanding our students as both emotional and academic beings helps us extend our understanding and development of their successes. Knowing our students as individuals is essential for us to tailor our tasks and assignments to meet their needs.

Assessment for learning, also known as formative assessment, occurs when we obtain information about what our students know prior to beginning a new unit or activity. By understanding our students' prior knowledge, we can gauge

- What information or concepts will need more focus
- What concepts need less focus because students already have a solid foundation in them
- Any misunderstandings we will need to address
- What connections have been made and which ones are missing

In assessing for prior knowledge, not only are we preparing for a more meaningful unit, but we are also telling our students that we value what they already know, that we believe they are intelligent and their knowledge will be important for the further learning of the whole class. We are sending a clear and strong message to our students that they are important.

Medium-sized Drive: Assessing for Prior Knowledge

DESTINATION

To determine what our students know about a unit prior to starting it.

SHIFT

By gathering this information, we can tailor the unit to meet the needs of our students. We will have a better understanding of what they already know and where the gaps are.

Explain to the students what is happening: we are gathering what they already know to better plan out what needs to be focused on for the upcoming unit. Empower them to understand the importance of their knowledge and how it can shape further learning.

UNFOLDING THE ROADMAP

Prior knowledge can be gathered in many ways:

- A class discussion about the topic
- Displaying various resources and having the students engage with books, artifacts, tools while you listen to their discussions
- Students can use collaboration software to share what they already know. This written record can be expanded on as they learn more throughout the unit.
- A quick survey or multiple-choice quiz that they can complete again at the end of the unit to show growth of knowledge. (Using interactive whiteboard clickers makes this a quick and easy way of gathering information.)
- In math, showing them two examples of a problem being solved and asking them to point out any noticeable errors
- Sharing only the front cover of a book and asking students to brainstorm what they can see from the image
- Asking students to record any questions they have about the topic. The depth and detail of their questions reflects their understanding of the upcoming topic.
- Filling in a map for a geography unit, using one color for prior knowledge and another color to add gained knowledge

CLOSURE

By delving into the prior knowledge of the students, you do two things: you show them that you are interested in what they already know, strengthening your emotional bond with them; and you gain incredible insight into where your class is beginning, allowing you to guide your students toward different areas that might better reflect their preferred thinking skills.

POSTCARD FROM THE CLASSROOM

Printing lessons are ideal for creating structure and routine in the classroom. It usually ends up being a moment when the teacher models how to form the letter and dutiful students spend the remaining time practicing this printing formation. It is very much a traditional skill and lesson, and it works well. I wanted to keep the peaceful practicing—but I changed up the instructor. Many of my Grade 1 students come to me with an understanding of letters and they can form at least one very well. To utilize this and empower my students, I asked each one to become the master of one letter of the alphabet. I then modeled how to do a printing lesson, talking the students through the different aspects of what I was doing. With this foundation, the game was in their hands. When it was time to cover their letter, students would plan and deliver the lesson. They would assess it (with help). They became the owners of the routine and brought forward many interesting ideas (dances, songs, stories). Printing became one of our favorite times of the day.

Use Templates for Unit Planning

We want our students to drive their learning; however, we also want and need an idea of what direction we are going and a chance to prepare for the upcoming weeks. Using a unit plan template allows us both the flexibility to follow our students' questions and the structure to know where we are going.

See page 116 for Unit Plan 1.

The template on page 116 provides us with the freedom to follow our students, using their inquiries as a main source; it also refers back to the curriculum we are bound to. It is the start of the journey and the first steps to map out the journey ahead.

See page 117 for Unit Plan 2; we recommend using 11" x 17" paper to allow room for the entire unit.

The template on page 117 is a much more detailed process in which we list the learning tasks that will be completed to link with student inquiries. The endnotes are a quick reference and check-in to keep us thinking of our students and designing the unit for them.

On the Road

Assessment as Learning

Ongoing assessment is a key part of student-driven learning. This form of assessment puts the student back in the driver's seat, as they are responsible for monitoring their progress in both marking their achievements and setting new learning goals. Students use feedback from their teacher and peers, along with their own observations, to help gauge their progress. As teachers, we monitor our students' progress to provide further feedback, instruction, and guidance.

While learning, students should ask themselves

- *How can I connect what I am learning to what I already know?*
- *What am I demonstrating I know or am able to do?*
- *So what does feedback mean for me?*
- *Now what do I need to do next? What are my learning goals?*

There are tools that lend themselves well to assessment of student-driven learning. These tools provide a snapshot of our students' learning, as well as providing our students the feedback and support they need to continue to grow:

- Diaries, logs, journals
- Portfolios
- Peer- and self-assessment
- Goal-setting
- Projects
- Group work
- Profiles
- Skills and competencies

Medium-sized Drive: Creating Collaborative Coaches

DESTINATION
Students understand how to provide constructive feedback to their peers (and themselves) when working in groups and as individuals. This step should be completed when the students have an idea or piece of work ready to share with others.

SHIFT

When sharing work, we often encourage our students to offer positive feedback. In the short-term this strategy works as we cultivate a classroom full of cheery high-fives and *Wow!*s. Eventually, though, this kind of feedback becomes routine and meaningless. For student-driven learning to really take flight, students need to understand how to provide honest, realistic, and constructive feedback to their peers. They also need to learn how and when they should integrate these suggestions into their own work.

SPARK

Is there such a thing as *perfect*?

UNFOLDING THE ROADMAP

- Share a piece of your work with the students—e.g., a drawing, a sample of writing—something that can elicit both observations and opinions. Tell your students that you want to share it with other people.
- Briefly reflect on the possible purpose and goals of this piece of work. For example, if it is a card, who is the card for? Why are you giving the card?
- Record students' comments on a large chart. Identify the importance of understanding the purpose and goal of a piece of work.
- Ask students to note things they observe about the work. Encourage students to observe both those things they like and understand, and those things that are unclear. Record these comments.
- Sort comments into two categories (use a large highlighter or actually cut the paper into strips around the comments): *What works for me* and *What I would change*. Working with the category of *What works*, encourage students to explain their thoughts by adding the *why*. Then move on to the category *What I would change*, again encouraging students to explain their observations.
- Ask students if you need to incorporate all of their ideas in order to improve your work. You might encounter some interesting opinions. Go through each of the suggestions and think aloud about why you will choose to integrate certain suggestions and not others. It is important that students understand the work is yours to make decisions about, just as their work is ultimately their own and they can choose what suggestions to integrate. It is also valuable to recognize that every individual will value different things about a piece of work. What works for some might be a distraction for others.
- Ask students to create a poster/document that records verbal prompts for *What works for me* and *What I would change*. These prompts could provide students with the sentence starters they need to help coach others. When doing any kind of sharing of work, these prompts should be readily available to all students.

CLOSURE

After modelling with a piece of your own work, use the collaborative coaching process with a sample of group work, and then move toward having students work independently as collaborative coaches. Continuing to add to the list of verbal prompts will help students create deeper and more meaningful suggestions to share with their peers.

Grade 5 students were blogging to determine what topic they would like to study for their project on humanitarian acts. This example models how peer dialogue can be an effective tool for assessment as learning. Tracking the dialogue with a blog, online document, or other tool allows students to visually see their learning: how their ideas are shared, how they are influenced by new ideas, and how learning grows into a new vision.

George: *war can sometimes be humanitarian aid*
Sarah: *george Libya isn't humanitarian aid*
George: *this war is*
Sarah: *no its not*
George: *Sarah if wer are helping Lybian rebels and Lybia is not Canada*
George: *so it is foreign aid*
Sarah: *we are kind of helping the rebels but it is not humanitarian aid*
Jacque: *assisting a far way country is foreign aid*
George: *Jacque do you agree that Lybia is foreign aid*
George: *we are helping Lybia not kind of but we are*
Sarah: *George maybe you are right*
George: *we sent planes to help in a coaliation a pilots*
Sarah: *I agree*
Davidz: *lets talk about the earthquake in Japan. And its about human aid*
Sarah: *that's true*
George: *we have to major thing to research on*
Sarah: *what*
Davidz: *maybe we should talk about Japan*
Sarah: *the earthquake in Japan needs more than humanitarian aid*
George: *japans disaster or Lybia's bloody revolution*
Davidz: *true but that's not our topic, we only can about human aid*
Sarah: *we could do both*
George: *that is human aid*
Sarah: *I know but japan needs lots of humanitarian aid*
George: *I do not think Lybia is getting enough shine in the news…*

The students in this group discussed and re-evaluated their thinking. Instead of a conversation, which could have been missed because there was no record of it, the blog acts as a record and provides an opportunity for the teacher to share and respond. Their teacher responded with this:

Compelling argument. You raise two interesting points—one, the humanitarian efforts to help Libya AND two, how the media coverage can focus our attention to certain countries/communities.   Look at the article I found on Libya and humanitarian aid.

Use Templates for Lesson Planning

See page 118 for a Lesson Plan template.

The Lesson Plan template on page 118 is for planning lesson activities. The prompts alongside the sections are to encourage you to consider how you are including student-driven learning practices in your daily planning.

See pages 119–120 for a Student Planner template.

See page 121 for the Student Planner: Independent Project template.

The Student Planner template on pages 119–120 is a tool for students to use to guide them through the process of creating their own assessment. The role of the planner is to focus students on creating a big idea and then making it meaningful. It requires students to look at the structure of their learning, to think about what they intend to learn about and why, prior to jumping into a project. It also helps them identify goals they want to work on during the project.

The template for independent projects on page 121 is designed to work with the Student Planner. It provides areas where students can map out daily objectives and reflect on what needs to be done for the following day. At the start of each work period, hand out these learning maps and ask students to identify the tasks for their work time. Having this organizational visual posted in a visible place in the classroom helps students and teachers know what everyone should be working on.

Destination

Assessment of Learning

Assessment of learning, also known as summative assessment, is the task given at the end of the unit to summarize what has been learned at certain point in time. This form of assessment becomes more complex in student-driven learning. The "here is the end goal" trap automatically focuses students on a linear path that they travel when heading for the same purpose. Quite often, this means the same task is given to a group of students for the purpose of comparative assessment: how did this student do compared to the class norm? Comparative assessment has its place, mainly in state or provincial guidelines. However, it's more important to ask: how did the student do in comparison to the goals they set and the quality of work they usually produce? Did they understand the big issues and topics behind our last unit? Were they able to extend their learning? Were they inspired and how far did that drive them?

DETOUR: THE TRAP OF THE RUBRIC

For many years, I was a fan of the rubric. My students and I would plot out the task and decide what the objective was. We would give it criteria and ratings, and the students would plunge ahead with the rubric in their minds, knowing exactly what they had to do to get the highest mark. I valued this tool. It allowed my students to know exactly where they were headed and it gave everyone the opportunity to meet the goal. But over time I began to realize that whenever I used this handy tool, all my students' work would turn out exactly the same. Each one could be a duplicate of the others' work. They strove to meet the same criteria, producing a similar product. But no one thought creatively or ventured new ideas. Did I toss out the rubric and deem it a failed form of assessment? No, I just had to become much more cautious about what criteria was selected, ensuring that it was more open-ended. I balanced this assessment tool with other options.

You Rule! **Project Evaluation**   Name: _____

Criteria	1	2	3	4
Content - Understanding of topic - Number of related facts and details	- Shows a limited understanding - Presents less than 2 topics	- Shows some understanding - Presents 2 topics in limited detail	- Shows a good understanding - Presents 2 topics in adequate detail	- Shows a very clear understanding - Presents 2 or more topics thoroughly
Communication - Use of words and visuals to capture interest of the target audience	- Much of the information is difficult to understand and/or is not in the student's own words - Visuals and text would not interest a ten-year-old audience	- Some information is difficult to understand and in the student's own words - Visuals and text would interest a 10-year-old audience some of the time	- Most information is easy to understand and in student's own words - Uses visuals and text in a way that would interest a 10-year-old audience much of the time	- All or almost all information is easy to understand and in student's own words - Uses visuals and text creatively in a way that that would interest a 10-year-old audience
Organization - Overall structure	- Final product lacks organization or focus	- Organization of final product is sometimes not logical or clear	- Final product is well organized from beginning to end	- Final product is creatively and clearly organized from beginning to end
Conventions - Grammar, spelling, punctuation	- Many errors in grammar and punctuation - Many errors in spelling which make understanding difficult	- Frequent minor errors in grammar and punctuation - Many errors in spelling	- Only a few minor errors in grammar and punctuation - Only a few minor errors in spelling	- Practically no errors in grammar and punctuation - Practically no errors in spelling

Comments:

_____
_____
_____
_____
_____

This rubric was used to assess a project on types of government. It is broad enough to allow students to choose the way they present information, avoiding the trap of everyone's project being identical. The students presented their information in a range of ways: digital programs, skits, posters, even interactive presentations for other classes.

Break Out of the Summative Task Rut

We all know the way it goes: What task are we going to create to assess our students' knowledge of this unit? What will the student create that will show their creativity? I know! They can make a poster and then present it. We have all been there. And there is value in creating and presenting information—lots of value. But too often we are too stuck in planning, assessing, meddling, and guiding to come up with a creative new vision.

If stuck in this rut, take these easy steps:

- Ask students what they would like to do to show their knowledge. This one question will elicit many new responses and ideas. I usually do a classroom walk-around prior to brainstorming to let them know the tools they can use (construction paper, play clay, etc.). The walk-around usually fosters many more ideas.
- Determine if the brainstormed ideas require significant background teaching or if they can be altered to meet the determined timeframe. For instance, if a group of students would like to put on a play while other groups have smaller tasks that fit the timeframe, present the play group with the option of monologues or a series of tableaux that take less time to prepare.
- Group students who have similar interests to provide support for each other.
- As a class, create an assessment tool students will be using to ensure they meet the criteria.
- Create a timeframe and visually display it, having the groups mark their progress.

- Meddle, meddle, meddle. Get in there, float around, provide ongoing feedback that is constructive and guides students to their vision.

ALTERNATIVES TO THE POSTER-AND-PRESENTATION ASSESSMENT TASK

Task	Description
Dramatic Production	It could be a play, coverage of a science theory, a comedy show using a second language, or shot-on-scene of a novel.
Monologue	A short piece written in character. Great for historical recounts or characters in stories; consider using background music and visuals.
Posters for a Purpose	Creating a poster that is intended for a specific audience, such as All About Germs to be posted in the washroom.
Models	Creating a small-scale version of a medieval village, an atom, or a habitat allows students to creatively bring out the smallest details.
Multimedia	The classic PowerPoint presentation can be transformed with tools like Prezi, embedded video, links, voice-overs, etc.
Artwork	Students create a piece that represents the learning, and then take the time to explain how it connects.
Booklets	A book, brochure, flipbook to share facts or fiction.
Charting	Putting the knowledge into a series of charts—pie, bar, pictographic—to represent the heart of an issue.
Songs and Poems	Using a contemporary song/poem and changing the lyrics to match the learning material, or creating an original piece that matches the mood of the work.

Medium-sized Drive: Creating a Teaching Tool

DESTINATION

To create a summative task that has diverse options for students to show their understanding.

SHIFT

Everyone has completed a unit of study and everyone creates a digital poster to show his or her understanding. While the posters look slightly different, there is little flexibility in the presentation and the information presented. If we open up the ways students can present their information, we can allow for many different possibilities and thus a more personal and creative interpretation of the work.

SPARK

Ask, "What is the best way to teach someone about your topic?"

- Prior to beginning the summative assessment, all students must have gathered and understood the information related to the unit learning goals.
- As a class, create a big-idea statement that defines what you believe people need to know about the topic/issue. If students are pursuing different topics, they will each create an individual statement.
- Ask students to review the information they have gathered: Does it support the big idea? If not, they might need to investigate further.
- Discuss the Spark question with the class and record the ideas. Encourage them to think beyond booklets and PowerPoint presentations: What about games? Movies? Cartoons? Songs? Stories? Models? Experiments? Photographs? Sketches? Journals? Poster? Blog? Website? Infographics?
- Go digital. There is a huge variety of online tools for sharing information; e.g., Blabberize, Bubblr, Bubbl.us, Captioner, comic makers, online whiteboards (such as Dabbleboard), Fine Tuna, GlogsterEDU, Mr Picassohead, Pixlr, Prezi, Queeky, Scrapblog, Scribblar, Spell with Flickr, Stained Glass Collage, Voice-Thread, Vuvox, Webspiration.
- Manage the projects.

  1. Define a timeline for the students: how long they have to work on their teaching tool. Determine the audience for the teaching tool: who is to be taught. Are there specific teaching tools that would work best for certain groups? Break the class into smaller groups and have each group determine two to three criteria for the teaching tool; the criteria could include everything from specific types of information it must show to broader ideas about the design. Share criteria and create a class list or rubric. There should be no more than five criteria to be evaluated.
  2. Students choose their preferred teaching tool and must create a proposal arguing the effectiveness of the teaching tool, as well as a timeline for its development.
  3. Provide students with a calendar or timeline that breaks down the amount of time required. Students complete the calendar or timeline by chunking their work into steps. Model the chunking with students to ensure they do not try to complete too much too soon or leave all the challenging work until the end.
  4. At the beginning of each work period or at time checks (if the project is being completed within a shorter window), ask students to identify their work goals. These work goals can be written on the board where they are visible to all.
  5. As each work goal is reached, refer to the class criteria to ensure that the teaching tool will meet the criteria.

- Share the project: Build in a brief two-minute reflection at the end of each work period. These check-ins will help identify any struggles students are having.
- Hold a Reflect session in which students share their teaching tools with a peer and evaluate their work using the criteria. Allow for time to adjust the teaching tools.
- Make time for students to meet with their chosen audience: their peers, a class of younger children or older children, their parents.

Not all summative tasks need to appear the same, especially if all students have been pursuing their own areas of interest. Creating a framework for students to use to understand the process of developing their own summative task allows for autonomy. Through the entire process, build in time for students to reflect on their progress. Help them use these comments to hone their work and modify their ideas. Try to allow this kind of diversity whenever you need a summative piece: if the criteria are clearly laid out, the piece can be different for every student but still yield the same information for assessment.

POSTCARD FROM THE CLASSROOM

This picture shows a project on the ocean created by a group of students. They worked together; part of that process was breaking into groups to complete different tasks. They decided to create reports, a poster with key information, and a display to share their ideas. They also edited and participated in each other's tasks.

Prompts for Reflection

Be mindful of which reflections must be permanently recorded and which can remain a verbal discussion.

In student-driven learning, reflection is an ongoing process for both teacher and student. It should not be reserved for a formal fifteen-minute reflection at the end of every unit. Reflecting on what we have learned and what experiences and skills we have gained from a unit or activity is essential. Without reflection, we lack the final part of our learning map—discovering where to go next.

Consider what prompts can create meaningful reflection in your classroom and try to scatter these prompts throughout the learning journey.

- *I learned…*
- *I accomplished…*
- *At the beginning, I thought… and now I think…*
- *I needed help with…*
- *I helped myself by…*
- *I have the following skills:*
- *I improved….*
- *I am confused about…*
- *What difference did my contribution/work make?*
- *I made a difference by…*
- *I was surprised when…*
- *What have I learned about myself?*
- *The most satisfying part of this activity was…*
- *Why was this satisfying to me?*
- *I think my most valuable contribution was…*
- *I found… interesting because…*
- *I found… challenging because…*
- *I was disappointed when…*
- *I was successful when…*
- *The biggest Wow! moment for me was…*
- *The most important idea I want to remember is…*
- *Where do I go from here? What am I going to work on next?*
- *I want to learn more about…*
- *Now that I have learned about… I want to…*
- *My new goal is…*
- *I want to teach people about…*
- *I think it is important everyone learns how to…*
- *This piece of work best demonstrates what I learned because…*
- *This piece of work was a challenge because…*

Become innovative with the ways you record and track your reflections; written pages that get buried in portfolios rarely inspire change. When students are reflecting, make sure to include your thoughts as well.

EXPANDING ON WRITTEN REFLECTIONS

Use these prompts and suggestions to take written reflections further down the road:

- *If you were going to write a slogan to describe this activity/unit, what would it be?*
- *Choose one noun, one verb, and one adjective to describe this activity/unit.*
- *Write a caption to go with a photograph from the activity/unit.*
- *Advice Time Capsule: On this strip of paper, write down one piece of advice for next year's class.*
- *If you could draw one symbol for this unit, what would it be?*
- Have students write on sticky notes to answer one prompt. Smaller reflections are often more concentrated efforts.
- Present a statement that students can respond to (e.g., *Fractions are important in our everyday lives.*) and have students stand on a value line that shows a continuum of opinions regarding the unit/activity.

- Record a class verbal reflection using an online tool like VoiceThread.
- During a larger project, have students keep video journals to document their process
- Ask students to take a picture of one artifact from the activity that they felt was meaningful.
- Keep learning logs in which students or teacher can write, draw, collect mementos from their learning.
- Using iPad applications like FaceJack or Funny Movie Maker, allow students to add vocals to an image to voice their thoughts about the unit.
- Ask students to sum up their thoughts about the unit in one sentence; add the caveat that their sentence must include the word "because."

Learning Never Ceases

Sometimes in our world, where we strive to understand what is right and what is wrong, it seems odd that we would go back to fix something we thought worked. But this is learning. And this is progress. A paper with checkmarks and a score out of 100% does little to foster an understanding of learning if it is not complemented with a review and a chance to take the next step forward or learn from mistakes. In our world of constant change, nothing is absolutely right or wrong. It is all part of the learning process and our role is to help our students continue to delve into the journey of learning. They need to be reflective learners and expand on what they already know. Our goal in assessment for learning is to determine what skills and objectives our students have achieved and what gaps remain. Learning never stops.

Unit Plan 1

TOPIC: _____

BIG IDEA: _____

FRONTLOADING ACTIVITIES:

TOOLS:

KNOWLEDGE BUILDING – *What do students want to know? What do we want the students to know?*

CURRICULUM OBJECTIVES:

STUDENT QUESTIONS:

LINKS?

Skills to be developed:

Emotional skills?   *Social skills?*   *Reasoning skills?*

Pembroke Publishers © 2012 *Student Driven Learning* by Jennifer Harper and Kathryn O'Brien ISBN 978-1-55138-278-4

Unit Plan 2

TOPIC: _____

BIG IDEA: _____

Start

UNIT SPARK

What interests my students?
What skills do my students have?
What are my curriculum objectives?
Are there connections to past units/ topics?
How am I checking for prior knowledge?
Can I include other members of the school community in my unit introduction?
Do I need to reorganize the room/ desks/materials for this unit?
What are other perspectives my students might want to explore?
What tools will engage and inspire my students?

FRONTLOADING

ASSESSMENT DURING LEARNING—ANTICIPATED LEARNING TASKS

What questions do my students have?
How will my students identify and explore the big idea of the unit?
Have I included time for student exploration?
Did I consider diversifying tasks for student interest and ability?
What are the different ways that my students will gather information?
Can I address any student goals through the learning tasks? Will students set new goals during the unit?
Is there are a balance between collaborative and independent tasks?
Where will there be chances for peer and teacher feedback? How will the feedback be structured?
How will I encourage different perspectives and new ideas in my learning tasks?
Did I build opportunities for check-ins for understanding? For emotional check-ins?
Have I included different forms of literacy (text, digital, visual…) in the tasks?
Are there opportunities to make connections to other topics/ideas?

Wrap up

ASSESSMENT OF LEARNING— SUMMATIVE TASK(S)

Does the summative reflect student interests and skills?
Have I included a range of choice?
What are the criteria for assessment(s)? Have my students been included in choosing the criteria?
Do the assessment objectives connect to the big idea?
How will I include peer reflection?
How will students reflect on their learning?
Did I provide opportunities for re-teaching and revisiting skills and concepts?

Pembroke Publishers © 2012 *Student Driven Learning* by Jennifer Harper and Kathryn O'Brien ISBN 978-1-55138-278-4

Lesson Plan Template

Destination

_____

_____

_____

Spark

_____

_____

_____

Tools

_____

_____

_____

Unfolding the Roadmap

_____

_____

_____

Closure

_____

_____

_____

Next Steps…

_____

_____

_____

Student Planner

NAME: _____

TOPIC: _____

Who cares about the topic?

_____

What is the big idea I want people to know?

_____

How I gathered information on my topic…

☐ Websites
☐ Books
☐ Magazines
☐ Newspapers
☐ Survey(s)

☐ Images
☐ Interview(s)
☐ Field Trip(s)
☐ Experiment(s)
☐ Something else: _____

Who do I want to teach about my topic? _____

What would be the most effective way to teach my audience about the big idea?

☐ Fictional story
☐ Letter
☐ Advertisement
☐ Poster
☐ Mind map
☐ Model
☐ Song
☐ Poem
☐ Skit

☐ Blog
☐ Artwork
☐ Monologue
☐ Speech
☐ Broadcast
☐ Letter to a
    newspaper
☐ Article
☐ Cartoon

☐ Website
☐ Game
☐ Chart(s) or graph(s)
☐ Multimedia show
☐ Something else:
    _____

Why? _____

What tools do I need?

_____

Pembroke Publishers © 2012 *Student Driven Learning* by Jennifer Harper and Kathryn O'Brien ISBN 978-1-55138-278-4

Student Planner (continued)

BREAK IT DOWN!

If you are going to make your teaching tool- what steps do you need to do to create the tool?

_____

_____

_____

_____

_____

On the calendar, map out your steps to figure out what your goals are for each work period.

What goals will you focus on for this project?

Skill goal: _____

"Working with others" goal: _____

Signature: _____ **Date:** _____

Teacher sign off: _____

Teacher feedback

Student Planner: Independent Project

NAME: _____

Skill goal: _____

"Working with others" goal: _____

TOPIC: _____

DATE:	Step	What still needs to be done...	Teacher sign-off

Pembroke Publishers © 2012 *Student Driven Learning* by Jennifer Harper and Kathryn O'Brien ISBN 978-1-55138-278-4

Resources

INTRODUCTION

Hole-in-the-Wall at http://www.hole-in-the-wall.com/

Muzslay, Leigh (2004) "Beyond A-B-C: What Testing Doesn't Measure" *The Sun and Inland Valley Daily Bulletin*, http://lang.sbsun.com/socal/beyondabc/part_5/future_main.asp

Rose, David, Karl Fisch, Scott McLeod, and XPLANE (2012) "Did You Know?/Shift Happens" Version 6, http://www.youtube.com/watch?v=XVQ1ULfQawk

Searls, Doc (2002) "Natural Curiosity: Dr. Mitra and the Hole in the Wall Experiment" *Linux Journal*, http://www.linuxjournal.com/article/6116

CHAPTER 1: HOW TO PUT STUDENTS IN THE DRIVER'S SEAT

Adams, Karlyn (2006) *The Sources of Innovation and Creativity*, commissioned for the National Center on Education and the Economy.

Brown, John Seely (2005) *New Learning Environments for the 21st Century*, http://www.johnseelybrown.com/newlearning.pdf

Kitchen, J. (2005) "Conveying Respect and Empathy: Becoming a relational teacher educator" *Studying Teacher Education*, 1(2), 194–207.

Klem, A. M., and Connell, J. P. (2004) "Relationships Matter: Linking teacher support to student engagement and achievement" *Journal of School Health*, 74, 7, 262–273.

Levine, Rick, Christopher Locke, and Doc Searls (2000) *The Cluetrain Manifesto: The End of Business as Usual*. New York, NY: Basic Books.

National Center on Economy and Education (2006) *Tough Choices or Tough Times: The Report on the new commission on the skills for the American Workplace*, http://www.ncee.org/wp-content/uploads/2010/04/Executive-Summary.pdf

Robinson, Ken (2009) *The Element: How Finding Your Passion Changes Everything*. New York, NY: Viking Adult

CHAPTER 2: TEACHING PRACTICE

All things PLC (Professional Learning Communities), http://www.allthingsplc.info/

Bennett, B., & Rolheiser, C. (2001) *Beyond Monet: The artful science of instructional integration*. Toronto, ON: Bookation.

DuFour, R., R. DuFour, R. Eaker, & T. Many (2006) *Learning by Doing: A Handbook for Professional Learning Communities at Work*. Bloomington, IN: Solution Tree.

Ekwall, Eldon (1974) *Average Retention Rates Related to Student Engagement* (chart adapted from information found at http://rapps.pbworks.com/f/ASLI+PD+PROTOCOLS+JUNE+3.pdf).

Holt, John (1981) *Teach Your Own*. New York, NY: Delacorte Press

Palmer, Parker (2007) *The Courage to Teach*. Mississauga, ON: Jossey-Bass.

Powerful Learning Practice, http://plpnetwork.com/blog/

Wiggins, Grant and Jay McTighe (2005) *Understanding by Design*. Don Mills, ON: Pearson.

Zhao, Young (2012) *World Class Learners: Educating Creative and Entrepreneurial Students*. Thousand Oaks, CA: Corwin

CHAPTER 3: KNOWING OUR STUDENTS

Aspy, D and Roebuck, F. (1977) *Kids Don't Learn from People They Don't Like*. Amherst, MA: Human Resources Development Press.

Coles, M., C. White, and P. Brown (2003) *Learning to Learn: Student Activities for Developing Work, Study and Exam Writing Skills*. Markham, ON: Pembroke.

Dweck, Carol (2006) *Mindset: The New Psychology of Success*. Mississauga, ON: Random House.

Gardner, Howard (1993) *Frames of Mind: The Theory of Multiple Intelligences*. New York, NY: Basic Books.

Goleman, Daniel (2005) *Emotional Intelligence: Why it can matter more than IQ*. New York, NY: Bantam Books.

Hattie, John (2008) *Visible Learning: A Synthesis of Over 800 Meta-Analyses Relating to Achievement*. New York, NY: Routledge.

Reichart, Michael, Richard Hawley, and Donn Miller (2010) *Relational Teaching with Boys: A Professional Development Workshop*, http://www.theibsc.org/uploaded/IBSC/Conference_and_workshops/2010_Workshops/REICHERT_IBSC_June_2010_PPT.pdf

CHAPTER 4: FUELING THE SPARK

Howells, Kerry (2012) *Gratitude in Education*. New York, NY: Springer

Kohn, Alfie (1994) "The Risks of Rewards", http://www.alfiekohn.org/teaching/ror.htm

McCullough, David Jr (2012) Commencement speech, excerpt reprinted courtesy of http://theswellesleyreport.com/2012/06/wellesley-high-grads-told-youre-not-special/

Meyer, Paul (2006) *Attitude is Everything*. Merced, CA: The Leading Edge Publishing Company.

Ogle, D.M. (1986) "K-W-L: A teaching model that develops active reading of expository text" *Reading Teacher*, 39, 564–570.

Papert, Seymour (nd) "Hard Fun" http://www.papert.org/articles/HardFun.html

Palmer, Parker (2007) *The Courage to Teach*. Mississauga, ON: Jossey-Bass.

Pearson, Kathy (2010) *Teaching in Troubled Times*. Markham, ON: Pembroke.

CHAPTER 5: GETTING OFF THE LINEAR PATH

Booth, David (2008) *It's Critical*. Markham, ON: Pembroke.

Classroom Architect, http://classroom.4teachers.org/

Holt, John (1995) *How Children Learn*. New York, NY: Da Capo Press.

McGinty, Frank (2003) *Take the Sting out of Study*. Markham, ON: Pembroke.

Pink, Daniel (2006) *A Whole New Mind: Why Right-Brainers Will Rule the Future.* New York, NY: Riverhead Trade.

Pink, Daniel (2009) *Drive: The Surprising Truth About What Motivates Us.* New York, NY: Riverhead Trade.

Reynolds, Peter H. (2003) *The Dot.* Somerville, MA: Candlewick.

CHAPTER 6: FOSTERING CREATIVITY

Ellis, Sue (2009) "Creative Learning Assessment: A Framework for Developing and Assessing Children's Creative Learning" http://ec.europa.eu/education/lifelong-learning-policy/doc/creativity/report/cla.pdf

Lehrer, Jonah (2012) *Imagine: How Creativity Works.* Boston, MA: Houghton Mifflin Harcourt.

McWilliam, Erica (2009) "Teaching for Creativity: from sage to guide to meddler" *Asia Pacific Journal of Education* 29(3), 281–293, http://www.vcu.edu/cte/workshops/teaching_learning/2011_resources/sagetoguidetomeddler.pdf

Michalko, Michael (2011) *Creative Thinkering: Putting Your Imagination to Work.* San Franscisco, CA: New World Library.

Osburn, Alex as quoted by Jonah Lehrer (2012) "Groupthink: The Brainstorming Myth" *The New Yorker*, http://www.newyorker.com/reporting/2012/01/30/120130fa_fact_lehrer

Robinson, Ken (2006) "Ken Robinson says schools kill creativity" *TED Talk,* http://www.ted.com/talks/ken_robinson_says_schools_kill_creativity.html

Robinson, Ken (2011) *Out of Our Minds: Learning to be Creative.* London, UK: Capstone Publishing.

Shively, Candace Hackett (2010) "Dimensions of Creativity: A Model to Analyze Student Projects" http://www.teachersfirst.com/istecre8/index.cfm

TED: Ideas Worth Spreading, http://www.ted.com/talks

Treffinger, Donald, Grover Young and Scott Isaksen (1998) "Brainstorming: Some Myths and Realities" http://www.creativelearning.com/images/stories/freePDFs/BrainstormingMyths.pdf

CHAPTER 7: DIGGING DEEPER

Barell, John (2007) *Why Are School Buses Yellow?: Teaching for Inquiry, Pre-K to 5.* Thousand Oaks, CA: Corwin Press Inc.

Bennett, Barrie (2009) *Graphic Intelligence.* Ajax, ON: Bookation.

Dewey, John (1910) *How We Think.* Lexington, MA: D.C. Heath.

Glaser, Edward (1941) *An Experiment in the Development of Critical Thinking.* New York, NY: Teacher's College, Columbia University Press.

Lyman, F. (1981) The Responsive Classroom Discussion: The Inclusion of All Students" in *Mainstreaming Digest*, A. Anderson (ed). College Park, MD: University of Maryland Press.

The Kid Should See This, http://thekidshouldseethis.com/

The Thinking Consortium, http://www.tc2.ca/

Willingham, Daniel (2010) *Why Don't Students Like School?* Mississauga, ON: Jossey-Bass.

Zwiers, Jeff and Maria Crawford (2011) *Academic Conversations: Classroom talk that fosters critical thinking and understandings.* Markham, ON: Pembroke.

Barell, John (2012) *How do we know they're getting better? Assessment for 21st Century Minds.* Thousand Oaks, CA: Corwin Press Inc.

Carter, Forrest (1987) *The Education of Little Tree.* Albuquerque, NM: University of New Mexico Press.

Donohue, Lisa (2010) *Keepin' it Real: Integrating new literacies with classroom practice.* Markham, ON: Pembroke.

Hattie, John (2011) *Visible Learning for teachers: Maximizing Impact on Learning.* New York, NY: Routledge.

Thurman, Mark and Emily Hearn (2010) *Get Graphic! Using storyboards to write and draw picture books, graphic novels, or comic strips.* Markham, ON: Pembroke.

Index